Sexual Trauma and Psychopathology

Sexual Trauma and Psychopathology

Clinical Intervention with Adult Survivors

Shanti Shapiro, M.S.W.

George M. Dominiak, M.D.

With contributions by Elizabeth P. Hess
Barbara G. Orrok, and Kathleen Bollerud

LEXINGTON BOOKS
An Imprint of Macmillan, Inc.
New York

Maxwell Macmillan Canada
Toronto

Maxwell Macmillan International
New York   Oxford   Singapore   Sydney

Library of Congress Cataloging-in-Publication Data

Shapiro, Shanti.
    Sexual trauma and psychopathology : clinical intervention with
adult survivors / Shanti Shapiro, George M. Dominiak : with
contributions by Elizabeth P. Hess, Barbara G. Orrok, and Kathleen Bollerud.
     p. cm.
    Includes bibliographical references and index.
    ISBN 0-669-27357-0
    1. Adult child sexual abuse victims. I. Dominiak, George M.
II. Title.
    [DNLM: 1.Child Abuse, Sexual—psychology. 2. Child of Impaired
Parents—psychology. 3. Incest—psychology. 4. Psychotherapy—
methods. WM 420 S5287s]
RC569.5.A28S5 1992
616.85'82239—dc20
DNLM/DLC
for Library of Congress   92-25642
                                              CIP

Lexington Books
An Imprint of Macmillan, Inc.
866 Third Avenue, New York, N.Y. 10022

Maxwell Macmillan Canada, Inc.
1200 Eglinton Avenue East
Suite 200
Don Mills, Ontario M3C 3N1

Macmillan, Inc. is part of the Maxwell Communication Group of Companies.

Printed in the United States of America

printing number
     3   4   5   6   7   8   9   10

To Cecylia, Ludwik, Frances, and Paul

Contents

Foreword

Suzanne Sgroi

Psychohistorians in the third millenium, taking a backward look at current beliefs about helping victims of psychological trauma, may be puzzled by what they find. In the last decade of the twentieth century, there appears to be a curious reluctance to assimilate all that we have learned about psychological responses to severe trauma since "shell shock" first was described in World War I veterans. Few academic programs in psychiatry, psychology, social work, medicine, nursing, or counseling place much emphasis on training their students to understand and work with trauma victims. Health and mental health professionals who are interested in working with this population still tend to find themselves isolated and away from the mainstream of conventional psychiatric or psychological thinking and practice.

It is within this milieu that *Sexual Trauma and Psychopathology: Clinical Intervention with Adult Survivors* can be most appreciated. Shanti Shapiro and George Dominiak, and their contributors Elizabeth Hess, Barbara Orrok, and Kathleen Bollerud, are all seasoned clinicians who have worked many years with severely traumatized victims of childhood sexual abuse. Their observations on helping such patients are thoughtful and insightful; all of their clinical suggestions and recommendations are worthwhile.

This book focuses on working with those survivors of sexual trauma who manifest serious psychiatric disturbances and sometimes require hospitalization. Some, but not all, of these adult survivors have severe substance-abuse problems. Some, but not all, may require psychotropic medications during critical phases of treatment. Most, if not all, overuse dissociation and autohypnosis as coping mechanisms, not only in response to severe stressors but also to deal with everyday-life events. All of these topics are addressed cogently in this book, always within the context of practical clinical applications.

Shanti Shapiro and George Dominiak deserve accolades for compiling this material for practioners. More, they deserve thanks from the many clinicians who have needed such a book and been unable to find it.

Clinicians in the field must cope with challenges emanating daily from patients who do not respond to traditional approaches. That is what makes this book so necessary. The bonus is that it is thoughtful, well written, and extremely practical. Future psychohistorians may be perplexed about why so many of today's clinicians have had insufficient training in victimology, leaving them poorly prepared to treat severe psychological trauma. But if in the future the psychohistorians have the capacity to survey works presently available in the field, the contribution of this one will be apparent. *Sexual Trauma and Psychopathology: Clinical Intervention with Adult Survivors* helps to compensate for the gap in our preparedness to treat survivors of childhood sexual trauma who badly need help now.

Suzanne M. Sgroi, M.D.
Executive Director
New England Clinical Associates
West Hartford, Connecticut

Author of *Handbook of Clinical Intervention in Child Sexual Abuse and Vulnerable Populations, Volumes 1 and 2.*

Introduction

This book has been conceived from a sense of clinical need. We have felt that the sexual abuse survivors we treat are not fitting the mold of those typically described in the literature. The patients with whom we engage are women (and some men) suffering from the ravages of sexual abuse, and much more. They are depressed, confused, suicidal, dissociating, abusing substances, incapable of attaching to others, or absolutely out of control and in need of hospital care. Except for articles and books about multiple personality disorder and borderline pathology, we have been unable to locate adequate resources for ideas about assessment and treatment of complex symptom presentations in the sexually traumatized.

As has happened with other authors,* sharing clinical experiences in informal discussions stimulated the urge to put our thoughts in writing; this book is the result. What we have hoped to create is a collection of diagnostic and technical chapters addressing the needs of sexually abused patients with significantly dysfunctional lives. The orientation is more clinical than theoretical, with an emphasis on the practical.

In sharing our clinical experiences, we learned that our patients did not follow theoretical paradigms. Each abuse victim presented as an individual with combined elements of healthy and destructive adaptation. The experience of prolonged abuse in most cases was devastating. Where repetitive incest prevailed, in some cases emotional, verbal, physical abuse, and neglect were also found to be a part of

---

McCann, L. I., and L. A. Pearlman (1990). Vicarious traumatization: a framework for understanding the psychological effects of working with victims. *Journal of Traumatic Stress 3* (no. 1):131–49.

past reality. This generally led to a legacy of secrecy, concealment, distortion, and shame. After surviving years of repeated trauma, breaking away from the powerful and sometimes life-threatening messages of the past is not an easy task. For each survivor, the therapeutic relationship was woven with its own personal threads of childhood representations, often recapitulated in the transference.

As clinicians, we know there is hope for psychological and emotional recovery from trauma. But providing effective treatment continues to depend upon many factors. We hope that this book will shed some light in this direction. It appears that the challenge before us as clinicians has been to employ our understanding of the workings of the treatment alliance in a manner that addresses what is unique in the patient while fostering self-respect and integrating fragmented personalities. It is not surprising that, time and again, we have found the cornerstone for clinical progress to be relationship dynamics. In one clinical experience after another, however, we found ourselves needing to extend the concept of "relationship dynamics" beyond the dyad of the individual psychotherapy. As we applied the term, it necessarily included the interface between therapists and other clinicians. Careful integration of the overall treatment and social milieu with which the patient interacted seemed key to facilitating personal integration and healing.

The book contains eight chapters. Several of the chapters are devoted to diagnostic assessment, while others focus more directly on treatment modalities and clinical interventions. Many of the chapters include case examples. Certain chapters are designed to focus upon such specific issues as suicidality, ego defenses, and chemical dependency as related to a prior history of prolonged sexual trauma. Other authors focus more directly on treatment-related issues such as attachment, hospitalization, psychopharmacology, and hypnosis. A number of chapters integrated theory and clinical practice. A common theme that emerges in the writing is the role of dissociation as being both adaptive and maladaptive in the lives of women who have survived sexual trauma.

Chapter 1 addresses the severity of self-destructive tendencies that emerge from the stress of trauma and the effects of forced secrecy and concealment. Chapter 2 explores the complexity of attachment formation in the initial phase of psychotherapy, emphasizing the clinical heterogeneity of trauma victims. Chapter 3 provides an overview of ego defense mechanisms commonly developed by the sexually traumatized. Chapter 4 focuses on sexual trauma and the use of hypnosis in the treatment process, while chapter 5 addresses psycho-pharmocology. Aside from comprehensively reviewing the utility and efficacy of using medications in this patient population, chapter 5 also includes a discussion of the psychosocial management of psychopharmacologic consultation. Chapter 6 explores the hidden world of incest in substance-abusing families. Chapter 7 defines the stages of treatment for dually diagnosed women with a history of sexual abuse and chemical dependency. The final chapter, on psychiatric hospitalization, emphasizes the importance of collaboration and communication across the boundary between inpatient and outpatient treatments.

Granted, the topics covered by this book are a select few. So many others unaddressed here equally deserve exploration, but will have to wait for a future edition.

We have learned much from listening to sexually traumatized patients. For example, the renewed and expanded understanding of dissociative processes and the enhanced appreciation for the importance of treatment relationships have added new dimensions to our clinical observations and conceptualizations of psychopathology in general. This means that how we experience our patients has been changed. Nonetheless, the limitations of our current knowledge in the face of the formidable challenge of treating the sexually abused is quite humbling, and perhaps it is also humanizing (which may be good for our profession). It is from this position of substantial uncertainty that we look forward to learning from the work of our many colleagues and future collaborators.

George M. Dominiak
Shanti Shapiro

1

Suicidality and the Sequelae of Childhood Victimization

Shanti Shapiro

Severe sexual victimization in childhood potentiates the development of parasuicidal behavior. The sequelae of child sexual abuse bring forth feelings of self-blame and a plethora of self-destructive behaviors that may be acted out in adolescence or later in adulthood. The underlying dynamics of severe childhood sexual abuse as it relates to shame, self-blame, and the use of self-destructive acts will be reviewed in this chapter.

Abused children who are brought up to maintain silence regarding the unspoken horrors of their childhood are unable to develop effective communication skills. The anger they feel toward their parents (or other perpetrators) is repressed and often turned inward. Feelings of love and hate toward significant others may not be integrated, and subsequently, close relationships may be chaotic. Because they lack an ability to modulate emotions or to communicate their inner experience, self-destructive behavior becomes their vehicle for expression.

Sexual victimization of children creates in them a sense of powerlessness, worthlessness, and an inability to produce change or gain control over their surrounding environment, even into adulthood. The act of self-injurious behavior provides a sense of control over their bodies (which become the object of self-hatred) that links childhood sexual abuse with suicidal behavior. It should also be noted that the combination of severe long-term sexual abuse, suicidal behavior, and level of psychopathology may be an important indicator of lethality.

Although statistical findings are important, this chapter will focus more directly on the clinical issues of patients who present with

1

suicidal behavior and a legacy of unresolved histories of victimization and traumatic childhood sexual abuse. When the patient's history of sexual abuse is undiagnosed, the related symptomatology often prevails throughout the treatment process.

Many of the symptoms noted in table 1–1 are commonly seen in varying clusters in adult victims entering psychotherapy. Goodwin, (1990) writes that "One might conceptualize an incubation period for the development of post-incest symptoms, mediated in part by the increased demands in adulthood for intimacy, caretaking, and integration, areas of functioning particularly vulnerable to the developmental impacts of child abuse" (p. 63).

The commonly repressed nature of early traumatic events may appear unrelated to the symptom profile at the time of treatment.

Diagnosis

When admitted for inpatient treatment, female patients with a history of childhood sexual abuse are often diagnosed with borderline personality disorder. Additional diagnoses commonly include depression, bipolar disorder, dissociative disorder, and more recently, post-traumatic stress disorder and multiple personality disorder. Although these diagnostic labels may fit the presenting symptoms, they neglect to set a path for the treatment of the psychologically negative effects of childhood sexual trauma.

The association of traumatic sexual abuse, self-injurious behavior, suicidality, dissociative states, and flashbacks suggests consideration for a diagnosis of post-traumatic stress disorder, because it indicates by definition that the patient's suffering is directly related to an earlier trauma. Severe childhood trauma and ritualistic sexual abuse can lead to a prodromic phase for the development of a borderline and multiple personality disorder. In some cases, the chronic stress of incest is recognized as a potential antecedent to borderline personality disorder (Herman and van der Kolk 1987). Many contemporary researchers have studied the high correlation between women diagnosed with borderline personality disorder and prior histories of sexual victimization (Herman and van der Kolk 1987; Goodwin et al. 1990). In many cases, the diagnoses of post-traumatic stress disorder and borderline personality disorder may overlap.

Table 1–1
Common Symptoms of Sexually Abused Adults

Acting out	Inability to trust
Blurred boundaries	Insomnia
Body image disturbance	Low self-esteem
Chemical dependency	Minimizing
Cognitive deficits	Multiple personality
Depression	Persistent anxiety
Dissociation	Promiscuity
Eating disorders	Reactive affective states
Emotional numbing	Recurrent nightmares
Fear/paranoia	Sexual dysfunction
Flashbacks	Self-injurious behavior
Hearing inner voices	Somatization
Hypnagogic hallucinations	Suicidality

Blame, Shame, and Self-mutilation

Although it is clear that a sexually victimized child is not to blame, self-blame remains deeply rooted in both the conscious and unconscious beliefs of the victim. Feelings of self-blame will generate a sense of worthlessness and self-hatred that permeates the developing child's perception of self and others (Shapiro 1987). The dynamics related to self-blame originate in the early stages of development. On a conscious level, self-blame can be understood by the manifest content presented by the patient throughout the therapeutic process.

A case example: Jacky is a thirty-three-year-old woman with a severe history of incest. Her abuse was perpetrated by her father and mother and began when she was four years old. Jacky reports feeling an internal sense of "badness" and believes that she is to blame for being the victim of the sexual abuse. She recalls the times that she went into her parents' bedroom and played a role in the sexual interactions.

At times, Jacky experiences being flooded by memories related to her sexual abuse. She is aware that her heightened sense of self-blame and humiliation has fueled her past suicide attempts. Jacky often verbalized that she wanted to end her life so that she could obtain relief from the psychological and emotional pain.

The components of unconscious self-blame have distinct developmental precursors that may be reactivated and intensified at later stages of development, including adulthood. Self-blame should be considered as linked to the earliest onset of feelings of both guilt and shame. A developmental framework suggested by Piers and Singer (1971) views guilt as arising from the psychic conflict between the ego and the superego, and shame as deriving from the conflict between the ego and the ego ideal, depicting failure to develop the ego ideal. Shame is a profound affect developing at a more primitive state than guilt. Subsequent psychological implications of shame are difficult to resolve, particularly when severe experiences of sexual trauma further validate negative self-perceptions.

Morrison (1989) suggests that guilt predominates in neurosis, and that shame predominates in narcissistic states. Sexual trauma cultivates narcissistic wounds that can lead to humiliation and despair, thus intensifying the experience of shame. The centrality of shame as it relates to suicide and self-multilating behavior may be an important factor in assessing lethality.

The act of mutilating oneself can be a patient's attempt to end the residue of emotions connected to the experience of intolerable levels of shame. The distinction between shame and guilt is summarized by Fisher (1985), who suggests that guilt is a feeling that surfaces from the experience of having done something bad, whereas shame is more directly experienced as an internalized sense of *being* bad. The severely victimized child experiences shame because of the perceived experiences of betrayal, loss, exposure, and humiliation by the abusive parents or parental figures.

Parental messages given to the child to maintain silence regarding the abuse deepens the internalization of shame and fosters the development of a false self to present to the world. Thus, the real self, burdened by shame, will fight to remain hidden from the world and subsequently from the therapist within the context of treatment. The fact that guilt, on the other hand, is not linked to the fear of exposure will allow the patient the opportunity to share guilt-related experiences with the therapist.

Young children who have experienced traumatic, repeated sexual abuse must repress these experiences, because they cannot effectively maintain the integration that would allow them to tolerate their unbearable feelings of shame (Miller 1986). The consistent messages about love, sex, and betrayal by the parent in cases of incest add to the vicissitudes of intrapsychic conflicts and flaws the necessary components of positive narcissism. This leaves the victim with a severely damaged self-representation that can permeate throughout adulthood.

Fueled by the intense inner experience of shame and the continued experiences of abuse, the child's perception of being damaged and worthless increases along with self-hatred and bodily disgust. When these emotions prevail into adulthood, suicidal ideation and actions predominate as feelings of rage and self-blame are directed toward the self. The inner conflicts resulting from unresolved shame build with each experience of sexual exploitation and add to the development of shame-induced psychopathology.

When the patient states, for example, that she no longer blames herself for the events related to her earlier sexual trauma, yet continues the self-mutilating behavior, the deeper elements of shame and its relation to unconscious self-blame must be explored through dream material and hypnosis or sodium amytal interviews. Shame, unlike guilt, does not heal by confession alone (Alonso 1990). The patient needs empathy, forgiveness, and true acceptance by the therapist to begin to shed the layers of shame related to a history of severe sexual trauma. According to Fisher (1985), the goal of healing is not to become shame free, but to live one's life undetermined by shame.

Shame is inherent in feelings of bodily disgust and self-hatred. Sgroi (1982) used the term *damaged-goods syndrome* to describe how sexually abused children and adults experience themselves in relationship to their victimization. Many victims of sexual abuse talk about "feeling dirty" and hating their bodies as a result of their past sexual abuse. It is not uncommon in inpatient settings to find women who have mutilated their breasts and vagina with razor blades and pieces of glass as a result of intolerable feelings of bodily loathing, self-hatred, and internalization of the victim and the victimizer. The body becomes the transitional object upon which the negative perceptions of self are acted out by the patient. These bodily acts enable the patient to be both the abuser and the abused. Most often, the patient will enter either a micropsychotic or dissociative state prior to severe acts of self-injurious behavior.

Women who have a history of incest, self-mutilation, and unresolved emotions of shame and guilt often struggle with intolerable psychic tension that leads to dissociative states. The act of cutting becomes compelling, because it serves to dispel the dissociative state and to provide temporary relief from the intensity of the psychic and emotional pain. In this context, self-mutilation should not always be viewed as a suicidal act. Farberow (1980) suggests a distinct division between "indirect self-destructive behavior" and "direct self-destructive behavior." Podvoll (1969) creates a distinction between deliberate (deep lacerations) and delicate (scratching) forms of self-mutilating behavior. The indirect and delicate forms of self-mutilating behavior often serve as a pathological defense and, in most cases, are not indicative of a suicide attempt.

The correlation between early experiences of continued sexual trauma, severe psychopathology, and the more deliberate forms of self-destructive behavior is well documented in the literature (de-Young 1982; Shapiro 1987; Walsh and Rosen 1988). All acts of self-destructive behavior should be taken seriously, and the underlying dynamics related to self-abuse explored throughout the course of treatment. The continuation of self-injurious behavior can become lethal if untreated. When struggling with a destructive alter ego (as in the case of multiple personality disorder) or extreme fugue or dissociative states, the patient may be at a higher risk for suicide. Use of crisis intervention centers and hospitals may be indicated for patients who tend to dissociate and suffer from brief psychotic episodes and continue to demonstrate suicidal behavior.

Dissociative States

The child who is a victim of severe sexual abuse can utilize dissociation as a protective defense against the horrifying reality, which is too intolerable to be maintained psychologically or emotionally. While the abuse is taking place, there is no physical way for the child to escape the situation. She learns that she is both powerless and helpless. The mind, however, is very powerful; under sufficient torture, alternative states of consciousness can become activated. Dissociation can, in an effort to protect the victim, be a temporary distraction from the traumatic event when it is happening. Dissociative states are common for females of all ages who have histories of severe sexual trauma stemming from childhood.

It is important for the therapist to inquire from dissociative patients how the process of dissociation was developed and what functions it serves presently in their life. For example, while under hypnosis, Joan talked in detail about an island that served as a safe mental retreat when she was being forced to have sex repeatedly with her father and older brother. At other times, she visualized herself flying outside of the house until the sexual encounters had ended. When under considerable stress in her life as an adult, Joan's dissociation led to paranoid states in which she had difficulty differentiating her husband from her father. This occurred when she was actively working on incest-related material, and she was flooded with flashbacks.

In a later phase of her treatment, Joan, as with many other women who dissociate, became an excellent candidate for hypnosis. The hypnosis provided a means of controlling the extent to which she focused on traumatic memories in the context of psychotherapy. Hypnosis was not initiated until Joan had developed a support system and appeared psychologically prepared for the grief work related to her traumatic childhood.

Lisa, an older adolescent at the time of extensive psychotherapy, reported dissociative episodes prior to severe deliberate acts of self-mutilation that placed her at high risk for suicide. Lisa described her experiences of dissociation as an autohypnotic state in which she felt helpless to prevent herself from deliberate acts of deep cutting, often to the extent of needing sutures. An important aspect of Lisa's psychotherapy was focused on development of signal anxiety to prevent further episodes of dissociation and self-injurious behavior. The internalization of the therapist as a soothing object also helped motivate the development of an observing ego.

In cases where childhood experiences of cumulative victimization exist, there is a connecting link between the severity of childhood trauma and the extent of dissociative phenomena. The use of dissociation, self-mutilation, and the myriad of self-destructive actions is related to unresolved conflicts. These surface due to the failures of repression and conflict recognition; thus, resolution and reintegration of split-off parts of the self are not obtained, and the self-injurious behavior can be perceived as ego syntonic. In certain cases, parasuicidal behavior presents a greater risk for lethality, particularly when the patient is focusing in treatment on issues related to severe experiences of childhood victimization.

Although self-mutilation is usually a nonfatal behavior that the patient uses to communicate her psychic pain, factors related to suicidal risk must be evaluated to maintain patient safety. On some level, the act of self-mutilation may bring a sense of comfort and relief and, as postulated by van der Kolk (1989), release endogenous opioids that produce both a dependence and a withdrawal effect similar to the use of exogenous opioids. Through repetition and association, the self-mutilating behavior is then reinforced.

When the patient is overwhelmed by cumulative traumatic experiences in childhood, ego disorganization, psychic pain, emotional distress, and intense feelings of anxiety continue into adulthood. Thus, the traumatized ego mobilizes the negative psychological effects experienced by the patient. The intensity of these emotions often becomes the precursor to subsequent dissociative states and the display of self-injurious behavior.

The following case histories illustrate the progression of psychologically negative effects of cumulative victimization.

Case 1

Susan was twenty-two years old when she entered a psychotherapy group for female survivors of incest. She was employed as a caseworker and was a college graduate. Susan's twin sister was married and had a chronic history of drug abuse. There are also two older brothers in the family. Tim is eight years older than Susan and has a history of violence and multiple substance abuse; Susan has remained close to her brother Jack, who is three years older than her.

Susan believes that the sexual abuse began with her brothers when she was nine years old. She recalls many fights at home during that time due to marital tension between her parents and the upsurge of Tim's substance abuse and violent behavior. Susan also has partial memory recall of being raped by Tim, but the details of the incident remained unclear in her mind.

When she was sixteen, Susan became involved with alcohol to the extent of experiencing blackouts, and her previously high academic performance declined rapidly. That same year, she began to be obsessed about suicide and started cutting her upper arms and torso with razor blades; she would occasionally ingest significant amounts of over-the-counter medications.

Susan had a difficult time in therapy attempting to verbalize her feelings. Despite her poor memory recall of the incest, she had vivid flashbacks and nightmares related to her earlier sexual abuse. At times she would doubt her experience of prior incest because of her fragmented memory of events, and this often led to a worsening of symptoms. Susan was often paranoid and suffered acute regressive states in which she was fearful of leaving home. She felt hopeless about her future, and her sense of self-worth was extremely poor.

Susan formed an idealized transference toward her therapist. She maintained long periods of silence in treatment, which appeared to serve as a wish for fusion and an attempt to gain ego recuperation from overwhelming traumatic memories and related affects. Burdened with shame and flooded with intolerable affect, Susan entered her first psychiatric hospitalization.

During her hospitalization, Susan was able to disclose her story to her parents, which enabled her to work through the denial of her incest. Susan was also placed on antidepressants while she continued in an intensive inpatient treatment program for two months. A one-year posthospitalization follow-up indicated that Susan was able to stop both the substance abuse and the self-injurious behavior.

Case 2

Lisa was seventeen years old when she was admitted to a residential treatment center. Both her arms bore evidence of superficial and deep self-inflicted cuts. At the time of her intake, Lisa said she had felt like "a bad person" since her childhood. She had considerable difficulty with abandonment and believed that self-mutilation helped her cope with loss. She also drank and used drugs.

Lisa's parents were divorced when she was four years old. Her mother was awarded custody of Lisa and her brother Peter, who is one year older than Lisa. As a child, Lisa's mother physically abused her by beating her with a strap and scratching her with her fingernails. Lisa was often forced by her mother to remain in her room for several days at a time. On one occasion, she was kept in her room for several weeks with only a pot for her toilet needs. Her brother would try to sneak food into her room.

When Lisa was five years old, a friend of the family attempted to molest her, but he stopped after she bit him. At six years old, Lisa and her brother were sexually abused by a baby-sitter, and the abuse continued for a period of one year. Both Lisa and her brother chose not to tell their mother for fear that their mother would retaliate and punish them. Several years later, when her mother was informed about the abuse, she referred to Lisa as a "slut."

When she was fourteen years old, with the help of her father and the court, Lisa was placed in a supportive foster home. Lisa continued to self-mutilate severely while she was living with her foster family. Prior to her placement in the residential center, Lisa's foster father died, and Lisa cut herself so severely that she required hospitalization. While in an inpatient unit, Lisa wrote a letter to her biological mother stating that she wanted to end her life. Soon after, her mother responded, stating that if Lisa wanted to kill herself, "she should do a good job of it."

Both parents believed that Lisa had an insatiable need for attention. Burdened by their own histories of deprivation, neither parent had the capacity to provide a stable, loving environment. Lisa was profoundly affected by her painful family experiences. She viewed herself as "bad" and needing to be punished, and "empty" with strong feelings of shame and worthlessness.

After a number of short-term hospitalizations and a year of intensive psychotherapy, Lisa began to gain some control over her self-destructive impulses. She increased her ability to use her cognitive capacity to recognize the onset of intense mood shifts that previously had led to dissociative states and self-injurious behavior. She made a connection to her therapist, and after several months was able to submit the following poem:

> Didn't they know words said to hollow eyes echo
> throughout the mind for years?
> Didn't they know sharp whips fallen on tender skin
> would soon dull a numb hurt?
> Didn't they know isolating a creative mind would
> crush a forgotten spirit?
> Didn't they know to ignore a sensitive soul darkens
> to love it cannot perceive?
> But did they know I was a child?

The poem was Lisa's vehicle for the expression of her inner feelings of pain and the beginning recognition of her vulnerable and damaged sense of self. Therapy was eventually a safe place for Lisa to express her inner sense of deprivation and her underlying and terrifying feelings of rage. As Lisa explored the issues related to her abuse, she developed a capacity to neutralize the rage and anger that she had previously directed inward. The intense feelings of ambivalence toward significant objects were decreased as she learned to accept empathy and caring. Lisa remained in residential placement for several years. She managed to survive through the many years of severe suicide attempts; her therapy will continue for many years as she continues to develop and work through the aftermath of her familial victimization and the feelings of shame that were compounded by her experience of sexual molestation.

Lisa is now a parent herself. She recalls the intensive psychotherapy from the residential facility as providing her with a vehicle for verbal and emotional expression of her pain as a choice opposed to her negative acting-out behavior.

Case 3

Although Jody was in outpatient psychotherapy, she had a series of six hospitalizations in a one-year period. Jody was a thirty-five-year-old married woman with two children when she had her first psychiatric hospitalization. Several days prior to her hospitalization, she cut her wrists and was contemplating suicide by carbon monoxide poisoning. The most apparent precipitating factors were related to a one-year history of severe depression and the initial discussion with her therapist about sexual abuse.

Jody maintained years of secrecy about her childhood and adolescent encounters with severe sexual abuse. Her resistance to addressing this topic with the inpatient staff was related to her inner experience of shame, worthlessness, and despair. As she continued to maintain the silence, her suicidal ruminations increased and began to dominate her thoughts. By maintaining individual staff contact and participation in a women's group, Jody eventually began to disclose her story. Some relief was noted, her suicidal thoughts decreased, and the vegetative signs of her depression lifted. Jody was discharged home.

Shortly after discharge, Jody grew increasingly depressed and suicidal. Her outpatient psychotherapy remained unsuccessful. Jody was rehospitalized five other times within a seven-month period. The reasons for hospitalization included self-mutilation, an overdose on prescribed medication, and one attempt of carbon monoxide poisoning, which was prevented by her husband's timely return home. Jody eventually told her inpatient therapist that she hated the hospitalizations and talked more about her inner sense of shame.

Jody's family was dysfunctional and unable to provide emotional support in her formative years. Her father was an active alcoholic, and neither parent voiced any interest in her scholastic or athletic achievements. The attention Jody recalls was related to her negative behavior. The parental expectation was that Jody would be a failure.

Jody did gain comfort and soothing from the many summers she spent with her maternal grandparents; after their deaths, Jody had reunion fantasies, which she disclosed much later in her treatment.

When she was twelve years old, Jody was molested by an adult male friend of her father's who eventually became her brother-in-law. She was raped when she was eighteen by two adult males while on a date. Jody learned to use her body as a sexual object, and her sense of self-worth and basic trust were flawed. For many years Jody escaped her pain with the use of alcohol, but she stopped drinking prior to beginning her outpatient therapy.

After marriage, Jody maintained a monogamous relationship. Eventually during her fifth hospitalization, Jody disclosed her story to her husband, as was recommended by her inpatient therapist. Jody had thought it best to maintain the familial sexual abuse as a secret, and she verbally expressed her anger about the disclosure. Jody had one last brief hospitalization in a state institution. Jody was frightened by the state hospital environment, was again angry, and pushed for discharge. Upon discharge, Jody was referred to an outpatient therapist who specialized in the treatment of sexual victimization. Jody had no further hospitalizations the following year, her condition stabilized, and the quality of her life improved dramatically. After several trials of medications, Jody eventually showed a positive response from a monoamine oxidase inhibitor (Nardil). As the severity of her depression began to abate, Jody was able to engage more effectively in the therapeutic relationship. Her profound wish to die was eventually transformed into a commitment toward life, albeit not without struggle.

At the time of this writing, Jody had completed one year of individual psychotherapy with no further hospitalizations. Focusing on the traumatic experiences of her past has not eliminated the suicidal ideation, nor the periodic episodes of depression. Jody is able to exert greater control over her impulses, however, and to recognize the role that her traumatic experiences have played in her life.

Psychotherapy

In addition to self-mutilation, other negative symptoms connected with a childhood history of repeated sexual trauma include substance abuse, depersonalization, nightmares, psychic numbing or amnesia, perceptual disturbances, flashbacks, acute psychotic states, and suicidality. When childhood trauma remains untreated, the use of psychological defenses such as denial and repression will be reinforced.

Denial, repression, acting out, distortion, and acute regressive states are part of the common defense mechanisms seen in patients with a childhood history of sexual trauma (Shapiro and Dominiak 1990). It is important to assess how each defense serves to protect the patient or to increase the risk of self-injurious behavior. For a more comprehensive discussion on defenses, see chapter 3.

Patients with a history of severe childhood sexual abuse and suicidal behavior present with highly complex and emotionally laden issues in treatment. The chronic nature of abuse experiences distorts one's perception of reality. Each traumatic event gives rise to cumulative ego damage and attacks the basic foundation of self-esteem, fostering deep narcissistic wounds. The residue of shame brings into existence intense feelings of anxiety and self-hatred, which rest at the core of self-injurious behavior. The therapist's ability to be honest, empathic, and tolerant while listening to horrifying life events can provide an atmosphere of safety and trust when the patient is ready for disclosure. The role of the therapist should be flexible and interactive. The therapist should be guided by the patient's need for ego support, reality testing, and integration.

It is clinically useful to obtain detailed information about precipitating factors related to ritualistic use of self-destructive behavior. These can become warning signs for both the patient and the therapist. The continued use of the therapist as a transitional soothing object will help to promote internalization and the development of an observing ego and the necessary signal anxiety to prevent acting out of destructive impulses. The limits and boundaries set by the therapist in regard to self-destructive behavior should be clearly and empathically presented; this can help lower anxiety for both the patient and the therapist. It is important for the therapist when treating patients at risk for suicide to provide protection, either by engaging significant others when needed or by facilitating hospitalization when appropriate. The therapist must be careful not to repeat the lack of protection that was provided by the abusive or neglectful parent during childhood.

The therapist must be careful not to intervene in a way that would induce shame or increase feelings of rejection or abandonment. The negative symptoms of self-harm can provide a temporary sense of psychic and emotional release from tension and anxiety. For some patients, self-mutilation may represent their will to survive, and they may continue to harm themselves until alternative methods of survival are available to them. As healthy narcissism develops, the need for self-destructive behavior will decrease, and more constructive methods of affective tolerance and sublimation will develop and become internalized.

It is helpful to inform patients that they can learn to control the destructive behavior and gain more adaptive coping skills through their motivation and the use of psychotherapy. As the transference develops, the therapist can assist the patient in slowly uncovering previously repressed memories and related affects. Linking feeling states with previously repressed memories can allow for discharge of pent-up emotions in a safe environment. For some patients, depending upon their ego capacity, uncovering repressed material may take several years. If the patient is a suicidal risk or if substance abuse is prevalent, the therapeutic work of uncovering repressed memories should only begin after the risk factors and the substance abuse are under control. Patients with a severe history of chemical dependency should receive concomitant treatment for substance abuse.

All psychodynamic treatment of suicidal patients includes a need on the part of the therapist to tolerate some level of risk and to monitor countertransferential issues as they emerge. Clinical training in suicidology and sexual victimization can help the therapist gain a greater understanding of the patient's internal and external world. Sound clinical training, combined with empathy and a desire to learn from the patient, will enhance both assessment and the therapeutic relationship. Throughout treatment, it is beneficial to support adaptive use of mature defenses.

Even when the patient is not at any apparent risk, the interpretation of primitive defenses and the uncovering of repressed material can create flooding of traumatic memories. When the ego is overwhelmed by flooding, suicidal impulses and behavior may increase rapidly. When the years of accumulated defenses to maintain secrecy begin to fail, the extent of emotional and psychic pain can no longer be evaded. If the boundaries are clear and the therapy sessions are experienced as safe and empathic, the ability to uncover the painful memories and their related affects will generally emerge.

When the cognitive and affective connections to the earlier trauma can be tolerated by the patient, a significant decrease in the need for self-destructive behavior will be noted. The goal of treatment can then become the restructuralization of the fragmented and traumatized ego, thereby enabling the patient to attain greater stability against negative impulses. Self-blame, excessive shame, and the use of self-injurious behavior can be transformed through the process of healing in psychotherapy.

References

Alonso, A. (1990, September). *Women on the Borderline*. Unpublished manuscript presented at the Conference on the Borderline Dilemma: Women on a Condition of Women, Amherst, MA.

deYoung, M. F. (1982). Self-injurious behavior in incest victims: a research note. *Child Welfare* 61:577–84.

Farberow, N. (1980). *The Many Faces of Suicide*. New York: McGraw-Hill.

Fisher, S. (1985). Identity of two: the phenomonology of shame in borderline development and treatment. *Psychotherapy* 22 (no. 1):101–9.

Goodwin, J. (1990). Applying to adult incest victims what we have learned from victimized children. In R. Kluft (Ed.) *Incest: Related Syndromes of Adult Psychopathology*. Washington D.C. American Psychiatric Press.

Goodwin, J., K. Cheeves, and C. Virginia. (1990). Borderline and other severe symptoms in adult survivors of incestuous abuse. *Psychiatric Annals* 20 (no. 1):22–32.

Herman, J., and B. van der Kolk. (1987). Traumatic antecedents of borderline personality disorder. In B. van der Kolk (Ed.), *Psychological Trauma*. Washington, DC: American Psychiatric Press.

Miller, A. (1986). *Thou Shalt Not Be Aware: Society's Betrayal of the Child*. New York: Farrar, Straus, Giroux.

Morrison, A. (1989). Shame, ideal self, and narcissism. In A. Morrison (Ed.), *Essential Papers on Narcissism*. New York University Press.

Piers, G., and M. Singer. (1971). *Shame and Guilt: A Psychoanalytic and Cultural Study*. New York: W. W. Norton.

Podvoll, E. (1969). Self-mutilation within a hospital setting: a study of identity and social compliance. *British Journal of Medical Psychology* 42:231–21.

Sgroi, M. S. (1982). *Handbook of Clinical Intervention in Child Sexual Abuse*. Lexington, MA: Lexington Books.

Shapiro, S. (1987). Self-mutilation and self-blame in incest victims. *American Journal of Psychotherapy* 41:46–55.

Shapiro, S., and G. Dominiak. (1990). Common psychological defenses seen in the treatment of sexually abused adolescents. *American Journal of Psychotherapy* 42 (no. 1):68–74.

van der Kolk, B. (1989). Compulsion to repeat the trauma: re-enactment, revictimization, and masochism. *Psychiatric Clinics of North America* 12 (no. 2):389–411.

Walsh, W. B., and Rosen, M. P. (1988). *Self-Mutilation: Theory, Research and Treatment*. New York: Guilford Press.

2

Attachment Dynamics in the Opening Phase of Psychotherapy with Sexually Abused Women

George M. Dominiak

A common assumption in psychotherapy is that matters of technique determine outcome. In recent years, with the increase in attention being paid to patients who have been sexually traumatized, case reports and clinical papers have begun entering the literature with technical suggestions regarding the psychotherapeutic needs of this patient group (Courtois 1988; Stone 1989; Levine 1990; Meiselman 1990; McCann and Pearlman 1990; Shapiro and Dominiak 1990). Though it is beyond the scope of this chapter to present a comprehensive review of clinical recommendations regarding psychotherapy of the abused, one can focus on a key component of the process: the early attachment phase in the beginning of treatment.

Working assumptions have developed about the nature of the difficulties that sexually abused patients show in developing human attachments. Unfortunately, there is little comparative empirical evidence and essentially no literature specific to the topic, with the exception of a brief biological and ethological discussion by van der Kolk (1987). In fact, regarding sexually abused patients, it appears that clinical lore has been given veridical acceptance. Since we have no research data, it makes sense that clinical experiences shared by mental health professionals be given such importance. This shared experience is the only "data" we have from which we may develop clinical beliefs; a few of the latter will be explored here.

One common assumption is that the process of attachment to caregivers is thought to be abnormally affected in the sexually abused because of repeated experiences of blatant violation of basic trust, usually by significant others. The sexual violation typically occurs in the context of absolute powerlessness and utter devaluation of personhood, which teaches the victim that even loved ones, family, and family friends can abuse. They are forced to learn that years of caring gestures and familial or friendly decorum may mean nothing if the loved one turns on you to exercise authority or power through sexual violation. Other nonabusing caretakers or friends are also felt to be untrustworthy, mostly because they have failed the abuse victim in not protecting or soothing her. In response, a sense of isolation and various forms of behavioral and psychological self-protection develop (Shapiro and Dominiak 1990), most of which interfere in the formation of trusting and genuine interpersonal relationships. The capacity for human bonding is abnormally affected, and aberrations in the process of attachment are thought to result.

When we as mental health professionals begin working toward creating a therapeutic alliance with a sexually traumatized person, from the first contact the interpersonal field is not power neutral. At the outset of treatment, it is implicit that we as professionals have expertise, special knowledge, and the power to execute our skills allegedly as helpers and caregivers. Typically, patients hope we have something to offer that they could not achieve without us. In the beginning, the relationship is uneven, with the patient subjecting herself to the power of the therapist's knowledge and clinically motivated manipulations.

Though overstated here for the sake of making a point, it is obvious how sensitivity to abuse of power and control and the inapplicability of implied trustworthiness by virtue of professional role may interplay in complicating the process of attachment between the abused patient and the therapist. In addition, negative experiences with previous clinicians and the various psychological mechanisms of traumatic reaction or other psychopathology (when present) will influence attachment to the therapist. For example, the dynamics of self-blame and shame as they influence self-esteem, sense of security, and feelings of social competence with others—all assumed to be altered by sexual traumatization (Shapiro 1987)—may be activated by contact with the therapist and interfere in the relationship.

Ironically, as sensible as the discussion just completed may seem, it is essentially assumption and hypothesis reinforced by bits of clinical experience. It should be appreciated as only theory. Serious limitations lie in the general applicability of these concepts to as diverse a group of patients as the sexually traumatized. Should we then disregard it? No; certainly, we should not be too discouraged by the limitations. There may indeed be truths in our assumptions that point to commonalities among abused individuals. In particular, our yet-to-be-validated clinical beliefs may guide us in learning more about how sexually abused patients attach to caregivers in ways that distinguish them from others who have not suffered sexual trauma.

The present chapter will attempt to discuss attachment dynamics of abused as compared to nonabused patients in the early alliance-building stage of psychotherapy. The purpose of this effort is not to compare "scientifically" the attachment styles of abused individuals entering psychotherapy with the styles of similar but nonabused patients. Rather, this considerably more modest effort will only begin to address characteristics in the process of developing therapeutic relationships with these patients that may influence our treatment techniques. Though some clinical material will be reviewed and presented as "data," the crudeness of the methodology will allow the reader to use the information only as a starting point for discussion and clarification of more sound theoretical and empirical approaches to these issues.

The Chart Review

The treatment records of forty adult female patients treated by the same male psychiatrist were reviewed. Twenty had entered therapy openly attributing at least some of their difficulties to having been sexually abused in childhood and adolescence. The other twenty were matched approximately by age, race, and nonpsychotic Axis I DSM-III-R diagnostic category and the presence or absence of personality disorder. To the best of their knowledge and the knowledge of the therapist, the latter twenty had not suffered sexual abuse.

Three styles or dimensions of attachment were used as categories into which the patients were nonblindly tallied: aggressive-hostile intrusive, quiet-suffering guarded avoidant, and affiliative–care seeking. The aggressive-hostile intrusive type is characterized by a demanding, devaluing, angry, and controlling style of interaction. The patient presents with a sense of entitlement about dictating the nature of the treatment and the therapist's behavior. The quiet-suffering guarded avoidant type shows the patient to be passive, reserved, and hesitant to disclose or share information. She may minimize the importance or severity of symptoms. Her associated mood is anxious, with sad affect. The affiliative–care seeking type of attachment is marked by a sincere and expressed interest in getting help from someone who is expected to be expert. The patient develops a dependent quality in the relationship with the therapist. She typically appears open to responding with effort to all clinical suggestions. Contact with the therapist is itself experienced consciously by the patient as comforting.

These three categories were chosen somewhat arbitrarily from discussions with colleagues and trainees as representative of common clinical experience with abused and characterologically disturbed patients. They were in no way assumed to be complete as a classification of attachment types. The hope was that even with just three overly generalized characterizations, some differences might be seen which could ultimately be attributed to the presence of sexual abuse.

Given the comments in the introductory remarks of this chapter, one may hypothesize that sexually abused patients would have difficulty developing affiliative–help seeking kinds of attachments. Mistrust of those in authority and a familiarity with isolation might lead one to hypothesize that a guarded avoidant type of attachment might be more common. Hostile attachments can be seen in various types of character pathology and disorders with paranoia. Though not rare in this group (especially among adolescents), hostile attachments are probably not specific to sexually abused patients. In summary, one would expect less affiliative attachment and more guarded avoidant connections, with hostile attachments interspersed in the groups in a nonspecific distribution.

The categorization of a patient into one of the three attachment types was determined by review of chart descriptions of the nature of the relationship with the psychiatrist in the first three months of treatment. Of interest, in many cases the relationship had changed in style during later phases of treatment, but this was irrelevant to the present task and ignored during the categorization process. In short, the method was that of the author simply categorizing patients from chart review into one of three attachment-style subtypes. It should be noted that the tallying of the patients was not based on subtle clinical nuance but rather on what was thought to be characteristic of the treatment relationship. The three categories were general enough that there was little uncertainty, though blind raters and statistical validation were not employed in this preliminary work.

The ages of the women in the review ranged from eighteen to sixty-six. Two patients in each group were black, one in each was Americanized but raised in the traditions of India, and the others

Table 2–1
Distribution of Attachment Subtypes Seen in the Opening Phase of Psychotherapy with Abused and Nonabused Patients

	Abused (N = 20)		*Nonabused (N = 20)*	
	N	%	N	%
HI	3	15	0	0
GA	11	55	8	40
CS	6	30	12	60

Note: HI = aggressive-hostile intrusive type of attachment; GA = quiet-suffering guarded avoidant type; CS = affiliative–care seeking type

were white Americans. Diagnostically, in addition to the presence of significant symptoms of delayed post-traumatic stress disorder in half of the abused group, the diagnoses of all forty subjects fell into four categories: personality disorder, recurrent major depression, anorexia/bulimia, and panic disorder.

The results (table 2–1) show that in the abused group, three patients (15 percent) manifested the hostile-intrusive (HI) type of attachment. Eleven (55 percent) showed the quiet-suffering guarded avoidant (GA) type, and six (30 percent) showed the affiliative–care seeking type (CS). In the nonabused group, no patients developed the HI attachment type, eight (40 percent) showed the GA type, and twelve (60 percent) showed the CS type.

A Discussion of Variables
Important to Attachment Dynamics

The nature of the sampling process, the number of patients in the various groups, and the method of rating limit the use of statistical analysis. Some discussion as it relates to attachment, however, may be useful. As hypothesized, there were trends among the abused patients showing more of the guarded avoidant type than the affiliative-care seeking type. A tendency to the opposite is seen among the nonabused. Significantly, one sees that the overall differences are not dramatic. Again, however, one must question the discriminating power of this methodology in drawing conclusions.

A few words about the women showing the aggressive-hostile intrusive style might be helpful. This group of three patients were between twenty-five and thirty-five years old. They were heterogeneous with regard to race. All three showed considerable character pathology and met criteria for borderline personality disorder, bulimia, and anxiety disorders; in other words, generally speaking, they were among the most disturbed in the group. Interestingly, one of the three did not suffer long-standing sexual abuse through childhood. She was subjected to one incident of incestuous contact. The other two were abused by their fathers in addition to other male relatives. It appears that the three were heterogeneous with respect to duration of abuse, relationship to the perpetrator, and number of perpetrators. As an aside, the hostility did abate later in treatment with all three and changed to episodes of horrible anxiety and misery with enormously conflicted dependency strivings toward the therapist.

In comparison, some of the patients in the nonabused group showed equally chaotic, though not sexually abusive childhood experiences. One must wonder if the absence of sexual traumatization could account for the lack of the hostile-intrusive attachment type in this group. With only three of twenty patients in the sexually abused group showing the HI type (a very low overall frequency), however, one could not recommend more than conjecture on this point.

A notable fact among the subjects of this review is that the abused patients came to treatment openly describing sexual abuse as a known component in their psychological unhappiness. The defensive maneuvers and clinical manifestations are often quite different in patients who present in denial or who have not yet become aware of the presence of sexual abuse dynamics or post-traumatic stress reactions in themselves. Given that, one might assume that the attachment dynamics may show a different spectrum of types as well. For example, patients in denial may be more prone to showing dramatic negative reactions to a therapist's comments and behaviors, with no clear or apparent explanation for their responses. Others may show unremitting depression or vacillations in mood that disrupt the flow of initial meetings. Actually, a hypothesis could be drawn from clinical experience with this group that expects less overall consistency in attachment dynamics.

There also appears to be a third group in addition to patients who have begun integrating and working through the effects of abuse, as in the studied group above, and those who are in denial or have the abuse experience essentially psychologically buried. This group consists of patients who have become aware but are not yet able to tolerate or integrate this knowledge. They may present clinically as overwhelmed by their own reactions to the awareness. If carefully observed, their style of attachment dynamics might be hypothesized to overlap with those who are in denial. Whether they become aware outside of treatment and seek help in desperation or recollect in therapy, these patients commonly suffer conflict between feeling a strong desire to abreact and the struggle to suppress and modulate their reactions. In crisis, they are nearly inconsolable yet direly in need of understanding, a safe arena in which to do the psychological work, and empathic sympathetic care.

Because of the mixed tendencies to emote and attempt control, the nature of the attachment to the therapist by this group also reflects this process by appearing to be dramatically inconsistent. The same patient may show fear, the threat of fleeing therapy, and self-destructive impulsivity, as well as a desperate need for caring and sympathetic human contact. Until treatment progresses over time, unpredictability in clinical presentation and quality of attachment may be what is expected. A patient of this kind could not be categorized by the attachment-type classification described earlier. Attempts at categorization would most likely lead to observations of equally intense frequent shifts among the three attachment types.

Also of potential significance in the chart review presented above is the fact that the therapist of the patients described is male. Again, there is much lore about the difficulties of male therapists being able to avoid the enactment of culturally bred sociopolitical power dynamics in treating the sexually abused. The "reality" of certain interpersonal dynamics being socialized into the male persona is thought to impede the male therapist's ability to meet the female sexually abused patient's need to develop a sense of implicit trust and safety with her therapist. As Courtois (1988) writes:

> The predominant question has to do with whether male therapists can overcome their socialization to disengage from a position of power with females and to adequately identify and empathize with the incest victim/survivor and her experience. Many feminist authors and clinicians believe that male therapists consciously or unconsciously tend to identify with the male perpetrator's position and deny, excuse, or minimize his behavior, while ascribing blame to the victim and denying or minimizing the effects of incest. (p. 239)

The issue of therapist gender is a complicated one, calling to arms arguments regarding clinical technique, professionalism, sociopolitical beliefs, and social activism. The ethics of blending political and clinical intentions have also been called into question (Lakin 1991). As in all debate and controversy, there is some truth in each position.

Taking an objective perspective, and considering the huge number of sexually abused women patients, one cannot categorically say that male therapists have not succeeded in helping the sexually traumatized. In fact, some of the leading clinical writers and researchers of treating sexually abused women are male, including van der Kolk, Stone, Kluft, and Friedrich, to name a few.

From a psychoanalytic vantage point, there is something to be said about either gender. In the case of male perpetrators, the male therapist/analyst offers a different (and perhaps normalizing) experience of maleness and the opportunity to work through suppressed or denied aggressive reactions to brutalization. Of course, with the unavoidable power dynamics lies the possibility of insensitivity, the therapeutic blind spots of male bias, and the potential for inadvertent repetition of elements of the victimization experience. Regarding a female (that is, opposite sexed to the perpetrator) therapist/analyst, other obstacles arise. With female therapists, the transference manifestations of the therapist as representing the failed maternal caretaker/protector may develop. In another form, the transference may progress to incorporate a belief that mother served as an enabler of the abuse via her failure to protect the patient/child. The patient could find herself doubting the veracity and trustworthiness of the therapist's comments. As often occurs, the patient might develop from this the belief that the therapist thinks she (the victim) somehow deserved the abuse or instigated it.

There is no escaping the unconscious or overt psychological machinations arising in the therapeutic relationship. Transference typically affects perception to suit the conflict being worked through. Over time in intensive treatment, details such as gender or appearance blend into the dynamics of the therapeutic work. In fact, the analytic literature contains many examples of descriptions of successful treatments of opposite-gender transference developments (Chertoff 1989). Transference is not typically bound by gender, especially as time allows the development of an active treatment relationship. In early stages of therapy, however, when issues of bonding and attachment are more prominent, therapist gender may be a stronger influence.

To this point, the discussion regarding therapist-gender effects speaks little to the clinical heterogeneity of sexually abused women. It appears to be applicable to the common patient profile/history of a woman sexually abused in childhood or adolescence by a male perpetrator; beyond that, it is unclear how to understand its usefulness. More often, what we discover in our work are very complicated abuse histories from which a linear relationship between perpetrator gender and reactions to therapist gender is not apparent. For example, many of our patients have been sexually traumatized by same-sexed perpetrators or multiple perpetrators of both genders. Others have had a close, emotionally protective relationship with a male figure, a grandparent or teacher who imprinted the possibility that feelings of safety, caring, and understanding can be gotten from a man. Also, certain patients have had positive experiences with previous male therapists that they seek to repeat. True, these further examples do not address the implicit dangers inherent in the psychological dynamics of the modern-day male therapist. The point to be made in the discussion, however, is an obvious one—namely, that the issue of therapist gender is not simple. Multiple influences dictate therapeutic developments and efficacy. Blanket generalizations about therapist gender should be considered unfair until determined otherwise.

Shifting now to a practical perspective, experience teaches us that female abuse victims in initiating treatment tend to prefer female therapists. The patient's choice, whenever possible, should be honored but not ignored once the treatment begins. Courtois (1988) suggests:

> The survivor needs to be in control of this choice and to have her choice respected. Her self-control was severely limited during the abuse, and an underlying goal of treatment is for her to regain control and overcome helplessness. This notwithstanding, careful analysis of the reasons for the choice both at the beginning of therapy and during the course of treatment is necessary. (p. 239)

Regarding the sample of patients reviewed above, one might consider the effects of a male therapist on manifestations of aggression in the early stages of psychotherapy with the sexually traumatized. Could this have influenced the presence of the hostile-intrusive attachment style in the sexually abused group?

The Question of Comparative Differences in Attachment Dynamics

Following the above comparison of three attachment styles in abused and similar but nonabused women, and a discussion of the variables of relative awareness and the degree of integration of the abuse experience as well as the influence of therapist gender, the fundamental question of this chapter remains no closer to being answered. Specifically, what, if anything, distinguishes the initial attachment process in psychotherapy with the sexually abused from that with nonabused but equally emotionally disadvantaged patients? Could it be that overtly the process of attachment, behaviorally speaking, might not be significantly different? Perhaps the overriding characteristics of the manifest psychopathology, whether from depression, anorexia, panic, or paranoia, are what determine the general nature of the attachment. For example, a depressed woman with melancholia who is quiet, withdrawn, anergic, disinterested, and nearly physically immobile might show just the same difficulty engaging with a caretaker regardless of her sexual abuse history. Similarly, the shame and humiliation regarding purging behaviors commonly seen in the treatment of bulimic patients appear to be present in significant intensity as a pathognomonic clinical feature in this "illness" independent of the presence of past sexual traumatization.

Also undoubtedly important are cultural factors that influence interpersonal discourse and sharing. To illustrate, consider the Japanese culture. In Japanese society, professional relationships are conducted with a respectful and quiet reserve. The reserve and respectfulness reinforce what is felt to be a clear boundary between private and shared information. Crossing the boundary and disclosing what is in the domain of the personal/private is inappropriate and offensive. One can imagine that a traditionally raised Japanese woman would find it exceedingly difficult to come forth with personal experiences of sexual abuse. Ingrained beliefs regarding intergenerational respect may limit the disclosure process even more so than in American culture, where greater openness and permissiveness regarding communication has not dramatically reduced the underreporting of abuse.

Returning to the topic of attachment dynamics, it may be that the perspective taken here is too broad. The three attachment types described above, and many of the variables mentioned as significant to the process, might be limited in clinical-diagnostic utility by their superficiality and by their generalizability as ubiquitous parameters of relationship formation. At the outset of this chapter, attachment was assumed to be an understood concept; however, some clarification of its definition may be in order.

Bowlby (1988) has described attachment phenomena at two levels. He and his followers have delineated many dimensions of the attachment process, but two fundamental categories are chosen here—those of "attachment behavior" and what Bowlby calls "enduring attachment" (p. 28). Hinde (1982), in reviewing conceptual issues regarding attachment and how it may be researched, describes attachment as "an aspect of a relationship with someone perceived as stronger/wiser which persists over time and situations" (p. 61). This appears to reflect Bowlby's category of enduring attachment; Hinde goes on to distinguish "attachment behavior" as being diverse and situation dependent.

As it relates to the present discussion, enduring attachment, as extrapolated from Bowlby (1988), may be a process so fundamental to human nature and the development of human relationships that it would prevail regardless of intervening experiences, even if the experiences are as horrible as sexual traumatization. Attachment behaviors, on the other hand, determined culturally and from personal development, are the visible evidence of the process of enduring attachment. Hinde's comments that attachment behavior is somewhat situation dependent imply that it may be inconsistent, malleable, and susceptible to becoming overshadowed by other behaviors under certain circumstances. Looking to find differences in attachment style between two groups of similarly psychologically disadvantaged patients, as was described in the chart review above, may be a futile exercise in that all one would accomplish is the confirmation of the existence of universal attachment phenomena and observations of our nonspecific repertoire of attachment behaviors.

It appears that attachment behaviors, the less resilient markers of enduring attachment, could be significantly influenced by any factors that would acutely or persistently disrupt the individual's psychological state at a given point in time. It is not surprising, then, that we often see in clinical practice how major depression, delirium, psychosis, intoxication, simple rage reactions, or the effects of acute crisis situations (which would also include revivification of trauma in dissociative reaction) alter the patient's available range of attachment behaviors.

Similarly, outside of a crisis state, or when reexperiencing trauma occurs as part of the working through of repetition in psychotherapy, the effects of sexual abuse (when not in the forefront of the patient's experience) might also be neutralized or overridden by the influence of the prevailing psychopathology. In contrasting diagnostically similar abused and nonabused patients, the observer would be left with little more than a comparison of the attachment dynamics of two severely disturbed individuals with depression, anorexia, or some other pathology, and no remarkable visible differences. At first glance, severe psychiatric disturbance casts a fog over individual differences. With time, elements that distinguish that person surface, and the interpersonal dynamics of a developing enduring attachment, with its concomitant attachment behaviors, become apparent. To summarize, attachment behaviors are person and culture specific. Their visibility may be affected by the psychological and biological state of that person. Enduring attachment is a fundamental interpersonal process that occurs at another level of experience.

This is not to say that attachment behaviors might not be affected by certain psychological disturbances in ways that distinguish that disturbance. When not overshadowed by other severe psychopathology, it may be that the influence of sexual traumatization may show itself in the therapeutic relationship in a manner not represented by the three-attachment-style schema used above in the chart review. From our clinical work, we know that working with the sexually traumatized patient "feels" different. There appears to be something that distinguishes how these individuals relate to us and, concomitantly, how they attach. As we begin working with traumatized patients, regardless of the uncertainty we might feel in the treatment alliance or our technical insecurities, the fundamental attachment process moves on. As therapists, we can sense it; the specific attachment behaviors, relationship details, and our conduct with the patient determine the nature of the treatment alliance. In concert, the experience these factors create becomes what characterizes our work with this group of patients.

Treatment Considerations

Perhaps, to better understand the distinctions we experience in the psychotherapeutic work of engaging the sexually abused patient, we must look to the details of the dynamics of the treatment relationship. For example, the intensity of the attachment, the content of the material discussed, the presence of specific sensitivities and vulnerabilities, and the relative tenuousness of the early clinical alliance in the context of otherwise normal cognitive capability may be the variables that more clearly differentiate abused from nonabused patients in the early stages of treatment.

I have already discussed above the affective intensity and potential for disruption of the clinical alliance that may arise as we attempt to engage certain sexually abused patients in therapy. Regarding the content of the therapeutic discourse, we commonly see cognitive recollections of the trauma experience and visual, auditory, and/or tactile intrusions of elements of the abuse into consciousness as "flashbacks." Also typical are issues of control, dominance, shame, humiliation, and sexuality, the need to verify caring as genuine, and behaviors that test the trustworthiness of the therapist. But all this is greatly influenced by the individual's general temperament, life experiences, ability to socialize, and intelligence, and perhaps most significantly by the presence of other concurrent psychological disturbance.

Many of us have experienced treating severely disturbed patients who have suffered sexual traumatization. The interactions between traumatic reaction and other severe psychopathology are not known. What we see in practice, however, are all the expected manifestations of sexual trauma, from withdrawal to vacillations in mood with destructive behavioral dyscontrol, but in an appreciably magnified form. Chaotic behavior, confusion, hallucination intermingled with dissociation, paranoia blending with flashbacks, and greater intractability of personal belief systems about self and others are common.

Fortunately, attachment theory lends us some optimism. Because of the universality and fundamental nature of the human need to develop interpersonal attachment, even the most disturbed patients, those with severe multidimensional dysfunction and histories of horrible deprivation and brutalization, retain vestiges of the human capacity to attach. Granted, in cases of psychosis or schizoidal character organization, the attachment behaviors may take such unusual forms as wanting to water your office plant every week or discussions of idiosyncratic topics. Nonetheless, the basic proclivity to form a human attachment (however socially peculiar it may appear) persists, though early on it may be difficult to recognize through the patient's unconventional behavior.

The task facing the therapist or caretaker is to find some way to be open to forming a relationship on the patient's terms but within clear, consistent, and reasonable limits. The presence of a sexual trauma history additionally requires that the therapist be particularly sensitive to the enhanced potential for misinterpretation and over-looking vulnerabilities in the therapeutic interchange. Clinical boundaries must allow for much-needed nurturance, but they also must be adequately clear to allow for an experience of safety and containment. This is a tall order for managing patients who have only a tenuous capacity to reality test without considerable distor-tion. The therapist serves as the representative of reality until the patient becomes better able to test her own beliefs independently. The attachment behaviors are unpredictable and may even be bizarre. Over time, the process of enduring attachment unfolds and may be-come quite intense and powerful. Within this intense bonding and dependency lies the potential for trust and growth.

With somewhat less disturbed patients, maintaining safety and modulating affect and behavior become less ubiquitous tasks in the early stages of treatment. The patients have a greater ability for ver-bal communication and safer overt expression of current emotions. Ironically, since the patient communicates less with action and more with words, direct observation of reactions in therapy can be more difficult to read. In other words, along with a better capacity to mod-ulate and contain reactions comes an improved ability to suppress and deny, and hence a greater possibility for interpersonal miscuing on the part of the therapist. For example, early in treatment, the trauma victim may want desperately to relax into a trusting position with the therapist. She may present herself as particularly engaging and thoughtful, in an effort to please the therapist, while actively suppressing feelings of being unsafe from her impulses and anxiety. Therapeutic patience and understanding the victim-survivor's need to regulate her own experience and reactions is essential.

Unfortunately, even the best of therapeutic efforts fall short. The affective intensity and nature of the clinical issues presented require extremely cautious and respectful management. When an error is made, the abused patient may react rather briskly with a rapid dis-ruption in the therapist's experience of alliance. It is the heightened sensitivity and reactivity in traumatized patients that is often misin-terpreted by therapists as a tenuousness in the capacity to bond. Early in treatment, only attachment behaviors that are relatively sit-uation specific are exposed. The process of enduring attachment un-folds more gradually.

Because of the apparent sensitivity and vulnerability of sexually traumatized patients to interpersonal dynamics, traditionally accepted therapeutic techniques should be reassessed in terms of their effects on the treatment alliance. For example, technical neutrality may not be experienced as neutral in the psychoanalytic psychotherapy of the abused (Jacobs 1986). The patient may feel hurt or confused by it, seeing it as an attempt to maintain an artificial distance. The experience of distance may grow into a misperception that colludes with the patient's belief that she is to blame for the sexual abuse, as validated by the therapist's lack of involvement.

Giving careful consideration to the effects of clinical activity is nothing new to experienced therapists. In the case of a sexually traumatized patient in the opening phase of therapy, however, the potential for alienating the patient from the treatment process appears greater than with other individuals. The sexually abused patient makes special demands on our work. Typically, she is astute in sensing unwitting or unconscious reactions and countertransference blind spots in the most experienced of treaters. Because of the nature of the horrors that abused patients relate to therapists, the potential for subtle reactions that distance the patient is great. All actions, ideas, or omissions of action by the therapist may be influenced by a personal response to the trauma described.

No one can be prepared for the kinds of horrors many abused patients so vividly describe and so powerfully respond to in treatment. To a certain extent, sharing in the memories and reactions of the patients is traumatic to the therapist as well. McCann and Pearlman (1990) have described this phenomenon as "vicarious traumatization":

> It is our belief that all therapists working with trauma survivors will experience lasting alterations in their cognitive schemas, having a significant impact on the therapist's feelings, relationships and life. Whether these changes are ultimately destructive to the helper and to the therapeutic process depends, in large part, on the extent to which the therapist is able to engage in a parallel process to that of the victim client, the process of integrating and transforming these experiences of horror or violation. (p. 136)

Our own capacity to tolerate and to adapt productively to this exposure to trauma must be privately appreciated and acknowledged. The challenge before us is to integrate our reactions gently—genuinely distinguishing them as our own, yet utilizing them in the service of clinical empathy—and to weave them into the treatment experience in a nonintrusive, honest manner that has predictable, consistent, and therefore safe boundaries. The reality of vicarious traumatization dramatically distinguishes the treatment relationship with the abused patient from those who have not been sexually brutalized.

Summary

Attachment dynamics occur at numerous levels beyond what can be observed behaviorally. At this juncture in our scientific knowledge, the attachment process of abuse survivors can only be validated experientially; we have no way of categorizing, comparing, or predicting it. What we do have are many assumptions in current clinical lore regarding the attachment deficits and dangers seen in treating the sexually traumatized. We must appreciate each patient as a study of one individual. Each therapist and patient enter their clinical venture alone, soon to become "together." In this process the frailties of human relationship become magnified, and fundamental expectations regarding trustworthiness are bluntly questioned. We have no answers. Our assumptions have no validity for the person before us. The risk is to enter the uncertainty and to work openly and bravely to generate a safe, containing relationship within which other therapeutic work (however it will appear) may develop. Curiously, violations of boundaries, relationships, and attachments are primary in creating the psychopathology of the sexually traumatized; yet boundaries, relationship, and attachment are what we use to heal it.

References

Bowlby, J. (1988). *A Secure Base: Parent-Child Attachment and Healthy Human Development*. New York: Basic Books.

Chertoff, J. M. (1989). Negative oedipal transference of a male patient to his female analyst during the termination phase. *Journal of the American Psychoanalytic Association* 37:687–713.

Courtois, C. A. (1988). *Healing the Incest Wound: Adult Survivors in Therapy*. New York: W. W. Norton.

Hinde, R. A. (1982). Attachment: some conceptual and biological issues. In M. H. Parkes & J. Stevenson-Hinde (Eds.), *The Place of Attachment in Human Behavior.* New York: Basic Books.

Jacobs, T. (1986). Countertransference enactments. *Journal of the American Psychoanalytic Association* 34:289–308.

Lakin, M. (1991). Some ethical issues in feminist-oriented therapeutic groups for women. *International Journal of Group Psychotherapy* 41:199–215.

Levine, H. B. (Ed.). (1990). *Adult Analysis and Childhood Sexual Abuse.* Hillsdale, NJ: Analytic Press.

McCann, L., & Pearlman, L. A. (1990). Vicarious traumatization: a framework for understanding the psychological effects of working with victims. *Journal of Traumatic Stress* 3:131–49.

Meiselman, K. C. (1990). *Resolving the Trauma of Incest: Reintegration Therapy with Survivors.* San Francisco: Jossey-Bass.

Shapiro, S. (1987). Self mutilation and self-blame in incest victims. *American Journal of Psychotherapy* 41:46–55.

Shapiro, S., & Dominiak, G. (1990). Common psychological defenses seen in the treatment of sexually abused adolescents. *American Journal of Psychotherapy* 44:68–74.

Stone, M. H. (1989). Individual psychotherapy with victims of incest. *Psychiatric Clinics of North America* 12:237–55.

van der Kolk, B. A. (1987). The separation cry and the trauma response: Developmental issues in the psychobiology of attachment and separation. In B. A. van der Kolk (Ed.), *Psychological Trauma.* Washington, DC: American Psychiatric Press.

3

Trauma, Ego Defenses, and Behavioral Reenactment

Shanti Shapiro

The main function of defense mechanisms is to direct the psyche in defense and adaptation. The employment of defenses is primarily an unconscious process that attempts to resolve intrapsychic conflicts (Laughlin 1979). Defenses are also activated to ward off or mitigate external and interpersonal conflicts, as in the case of victimization and trauma. Identification and clarification of the patient's defensive operations will serve as a guide for the therapist in defining therapeutic tasks for corrective emotional experiences in treatment (Shapiro and Dominiak 1990).

In this chapter, the focus will remain on the employment of ego defense mechanisms and their relationship to the aftermath of sexual trauma stemming from childhood and adolescence. Defenses subsequent to childhood sexual victimization may be adaptive or pathogenic; surviving trauma can lead to mastery or vulnerability and regression. The concern in this chapter is about those patients where the severity of trauma and suffering led to the use of defenses that became maladaptive and negatively influenced subsequent development and functioning. Another important consideration is whether the extent to which certain defenses are maintained facilitates the use of self-destructive behavior and psychopathology. When defenses become exaggerated, overly rigid, or brittle, problems emerge and psychopathology prevails.

Childhood sexual abuse is often devastating and may potentially lead to persistent negative symptomatology throughout adolescence and on into adulthood. As the abuse is continued, a complex system of ego defenses emerge in an attempt to master the intolerable levels of psychic pain, anxiety, and intrapsychic conflicts related to specific episodes of traumatic experiences. These same defenses that may initially prove adaptive can culminate in psychopathology upon maturity.

A major concern about ego defenses is how they are employed and whether their aims and goals are adaptive or destructive. For example, an adult who employs regression in a stressful situation may experience a reduction of anxiety and find a playful way to cope with stress. In this case, the defense would be adaptive. If the level of stress and anxiety is prolonged and intolerable, however, the use of regression may become exaggerated and lead to disturbances in interpersonal relationships and an inability to carry out daily responsibilities related to normal adult functioning. Many different types of pathology can be facilitated by exaggerated defenses that may have developed subsequent to cumulative traumatic experiences in childhood.

Consider the dilemma of the vulnerable child who is a victim of repeated sexual abuse by members of her own family. She is loved, abused, and betrayed by the same adults whom she is taught to trust and respect. In this type of situation, the child has no physical means of escape and may mobilize a wide spectrum of ego defenses. For example, the development of dissociative defenses provides a means of escape that initially serves to protect and defend against the psychological pain and anxiety stemming from the incest and the surrounding atmosphere of an extremely dysfunctional family. It is difficult, if not impossible, for mature defenses to develop sufficiently in the lives of women who experienced severe and repeated abuse in childhood. When defenses become maladaptive and exaggerated, it can contribute to symptom formation and behavioral reenactment.

The legacy of abuse and concealment fosters the use of dissociation, disavowal, and denial to push away or distort the intolerable factors of reality. Yet, stored away in the mind and body are the unconscious elements of the unresolved trauma, which is often acted out later in adolescence and adulthood.

The list in table 3–1 consists of some of the commonly noted defenses seen in clinical work with sexual trauma survivors. The defenses listed were chosen as a focus for this chapter. It should be noted that most defenses tend to overlap and reinforce each other. The patient's repertoire of defenses that are employed to cope with stressful situations contribute to the development of character structure and behavior. When immature defenses subsequent to trauma predominate on into adulthood, they will often lead to psychopathology and symptom formation.

Table 3–1
Ego Defenses

Immature	*Mature*
Acting out	Altruism
Compulsion to repeat	Humor
Conversion	Suppression
Denial	Sublimation
Dissociation	
Minimizing	
Projection	
Splitting	
Repression	

It is important to note that defenses by themselves are not necessarily pathological. Ego defenses in general serve to maintain psychological health and adaptivity. Women with a history of severe and repeated sexual abuse, however, tend to exhibit an exaggerated profile of defenses that prevent adequate adjustment to their external environment. Thus, relationships, occupational, and academic pursuits are difficult if not impossible to maintain.

The goal of this chapter is to guide the clinician in a basic understanding of defenses as they relate to childhood experiences of sexual abuse. Understanding the psychopathology with which the patient presents and the use of mature and immature defenses may help to direct the clinical tasks of the therapist in the psychological recovery of the patient.

Acting Out

For adults who have a history of repeated abuse, acting out is a particularly common defense. One definition of acting out is the unconsciously driven behavioral release of sexual or aggressive impulses; one can also consider acting out as the behavioral expression of repressed memories and emotions that cannot be expressed verbally. Acting out of destructive behavior can be directed toward oneself or others.

Powerful emotions related to either excessive guilt or shame can also influence and fuel destructive acting-out behavior. In some cases, the spectrum of self-harm can range from delicate scratching to severe and deliberate acts of self-mutilation and a myriad of parasuicidal behaviors. Acting out of destructive behavior may serve as an active repetition of prior passively endured experiences of early trauma. For example, chronic patterns of self-mutilating behavior may be linked to unresolved shame at having been unable to stop the abuse in childhood, blaming oneself for the abuse, or the experience of pleasure from the sexual act.

When acting out becomes a primary defense in which self-injurious behavior, promiscuity, and substance abuse increase the experience of shame, the patient may be at high risk for completed suicide. For the fragile patient who has suffered since childhood from repeated severe abuse, the shift from acting out to insight may be a long and tedious process. If the therapeutic relationship is to unfold, the patient must feel safe enough to verbalize the previously endured experiences related to her history of trauma. Only then can the need for self-injurious acting out be understood and eventually transformed through the context of the therapeutic relationship. The stance of the therapist, while maintaining boundaries and setting limits must also include empathy and positive regard toward the patient. The appropriate modeling provided by the therapist will help the patient feel safe enough to rework the prior experiences of trauma and internalize the understanding that she was not to blame for the abuse. When this can be accomplished slowly throughout various stages in the treatment process, shame and the need for self-harm can be greatly reduced and eventually discontinued. When the patient can develop an ability to tolerate inner emotions through appropriate cognitive and affective channels, impulsivity need not control behavior.

Susan was sexually abused by her brothers throughout her adolescence. She inflicted cuts upon her arms and legs for a period of seven years. She was unable to talk about her experiences of incest in individual treatment. A one-month hospitalization allowed her to separate from her family and to utilize various modalities of treatment. After participation in art therapy, psychodrama, and group, individual, and family therapy, she began to express the extent of her psychological pain. Susan continued in group and individual therapy for many years after her hospitalization, there were no further episodes of self-injurious behavior, and subsequent acting-out behavior was significantly reduced.

Compulsion to Repeat

The compulsion to repeat is described by S. Freud ([1914] 1958) as the patient's instinctual attempt to recreate, overcome, or master previously unresolved conflicts related to childhood trauma. According to clinical observation, however, the compulsion to repeat may lead to reenactment of traumatic events. In his recent literature on victimization, van der Kolk (1989) describes how traumatized adults continue to expose themselves to events that are reminiscent of the original trauma. This replay of earlier traumatic events has both biological and psychological implications. For example, hyperarousal, a physiological response to trauma, may interfere with the victim's ability to think clearly and to experience a sense of control in stressful situations. Many victimized adults appear to be addicted to a lifestyle of abuse. According to Harold Blum (1987), "Trauma is associated with a constellation of identifications with the aggressor, with the victim, with the rescuer, and with the caregiver" (p. 609). He views these identifications as crucial for the recovery and mastery of trauma. The psychological component of this addiction may be related to an internalized perception of the self as a victim and the internalized identification with the perpetrator of the childhood abuse. The compulsion to repeat revictimizing behavior can sometimes be equated with an identification with the original aggressor.

When a child is being severely abused sexually, or physically tortured, the abusive adult is perceived as powerful. In an attempt to gain mastery over previous experiences of learned helplessness or vulnerability, the identification in some cases is linked to the aggressor and to the experience of being a victim.

A case example: Mary is a twenty-four-year-old female with a history of repeated emotional and sexual abuse by her stepfather. As a child, she was abandoned by her mother for significant periods of time as a result of physical and emotional unavailability. In her young adult life, Mary was asked to baby-sit for a child with whom she formed a close relationship. One day while caring for the child, she became flooded with emotions regarding her own history of abuse and, subsequently, molested the child. Unable to articulate her own history of psychological pain and abuse, she reenacted the abusive behavior.

Prostitution and sexual promiscuity are often linked to a former history of sexual abuse (Burgess et al. 1978; Finkelhor and Brown 1985; Maltz and Holman 1987). Early sexual stimulation can arouse a plethora of negative symptoms commonly described in clinical literature (Russell 1986; Shapiro 1987; Stone 1990). Some sexually victimized patients may describe lengthy periods of sexual acting-out as exciting and adventurous. Their fantasy life may be filled with sexual exploitations and the desire to return to a promiscuous lifestyle fueled by the unconscious compulsion to repeat. Even the awareness of their damaged sense of self and years of self-degradation stimulated by childhood abuse does not always stop the behavioral reenactment.

Repetitive acts such as self-inflicted cuts, hair pulling, head banging, and other forms of self-injurious behavior as it commonly relates to childhood trauma are well documented in clinical literature (Green 1978; deYoung 1982; Shapiro 1987; van der Kolk 1987; Stone 1990). The psychodynamics related to the use of self-injurious behavior are extremely complex and are described in more detail in chapter 1. Bessel van der Kolk (1989) describes the relationship between endogenous opioids and self-harm. When a patient is repeatedly mutilating herself, she may be attempting to take control of her own body in her attempt to master her childhood trauma. She may also be dissociating, struggling with flashbacks, or in an acute psychotic episode. Each patient must be assessed individually regarding the etiology and lethality of the use of self-destructive behavior.

The process of recovery in the course of therapy may feel frightening and trigger the desire to retreat and return to the comfort of what is familiar, regardless of the psychological damage that may continue to result. As the therapeutic relationship deepens, and behavioral, psychological, and emotional equanimity is established, however, the links between childhood trauma and reenactment can be slowly resolved in the context of the treatment process. When the therapy is perceived as a safe holding environment, issues related to mourning family loyalty (in cases of incest), reassessing responsibilities, and learning new ways of coping within the therapeutic relationship can prevail.

Conversion

The defense of conversion permits the repressed trauma-related memories, impulses, and affects to be transformed into bodily symptoms. Loewenstein (1990) suggests that in victims of abuse, conversion symptoms can be noted in any psychiatric or medical illness and personality configuration and are not exclusive to a diagnosis of hysterical personality disorder. In several studies on somatization disorder, a significant number of subjects showed a history of sexual trauma in childhood or adolescence (Lewis and Berman 1965; Cloninger and Guze 1970a; Goodwin et al. 1979). Hysterical blindness and paralysis can be somatic expressions that shield the psychic anxiety related to trauma, thus placing the focus on the physical symptomotology.

Freud's early findings regarding the etiology of hysteria/conversion symptoms validated a positive history of incest in several of his patients. The relationship between sexual trauma and conversion is a common finding today. The following case example illustrates the relationship between trauma and conversion.

A case example: Mrs. Smith, a thirty-five-year-old patient, had reported a number of somatic symptoms. Her symptom profile included numbness of her left side and paralysis of her left hand and left leg. She received a neurological workup at a major hospital; the findings revealed no abnormalities or muscular atrophy. She also reported blackouts, panic attacks, and fainting spells. She was seen by a number of psychiatrists and treated with various combinations of anxiolytic and antidepressant medications. After several days of complete bedrest, the paralysis decreased.

Mrs. Smith's parents were divorced when she was two years old. She was placed in the home of her aunt and uncle, rarely maintaining contact with her biological parents. She did well academically and would routinely complete many chores around the house. She reported an experience of sexual abuse by her fourth-grade teacher, but she was told by her family not to talk about the incident after it was addressed with the school. Her aunt and uncle remained emotionally distant and, subsequently, issues of abandonment and loss were combated by denial. At age nineteen, Mrs. Smith married a preacher much older than herself, who also served as a father figure. The couple had several children. As the children began to separate from home, Mrs. Smith feared that the paralysis would return and was hospitalized after having taken an overdose of prescribed medications. Her primary defensive style was reported as rationalization, reaction formation, denial of painful affects, avoidance, and repression. Conversion was also noted as a primary defense that served to provide a mode of expression for the repressed traumatic memories of loss, abandonment, and earlier abuse through somatization.

There are many different kinds of experiences in a person's life that can trigger previously repressed memories related to a childhood history of trauma. The unbearable memories of sexual victimization and other traumatic events may remain concealed in both the body and the mind until the defenses begin to weaken and the truth about the past begins to surface into reality.

Denial

Denial is the disavowing or screening out of external reality to avoid painful and anxiety-provoking thoughts, wishes, or experiences. As a defense, denial acts as a shield against the intolerable and painful realities of the past. Denial is similar to repression, and in many cases the two defenses will overlap (Laughlin 1979). Denial is a primitive defense in adulthood and predominant in manic states and other forms of psychopathology. For the neurotic patient, denial is rarely absolute in its effectiveness at warding off the external truth (Shapiro and Dominiak 1990). Denial can block perceptions, affecting reality testing and behavior.

Denial of incest can be shared by the victim and the family. Threats, as we know, are often used to maintain secrets about the extent of abuse and dysfunction within incestuous families, thus compounding the use of denial. As the child matures, the denial leads to a distorted view of both internal and external reality. This can become the core of trauma-related psychopathology that manifests itself in adolescence and later in adulthood.

The continued use of denial can lead to doubt about the occurrence of prior abuse, heightening related anxiety through fantasy, nightmares, and flashbacks with themes of sexuality and invasion of the self. When the therapist is aware of the nature of trauma and related symptomotology, the treatment can become a safe place to open the doors slowly to the hidden reality previously masked by denial. Overcoming denial in the context of treatment is a slow and lengthy process.

Denial can also serve as a support or co-defense in conjunction with other defensive operations that can activate or ward off negative symptoms. Denial can play a role in attempting to resolve conflict or to avoid dealing with painful emotions temporarily while attempting to master specific tasks. The extent to which denial functions as a defense should be assessed throughout the context of treatment.

The following case is an illustration of denial and the impact of incest and alcohol abuse: Susan was thirty-five years old and a single parent. As a child, she was sexually abused by her uncle over a period of nine years. When she disclosed the abuse to her mother, she was not believed and subsequently over the years began to deny the emotional impact of the abuse. As she matured in years, she would use alcohol to escape from the intolerable memories. When she first entered treatment, she also denied the extent to which alcohol controlled her life. In one session, Susan began to focus on her history of incest. One week later, she began drinking heavily and was hospitalized for detoxification.

Both the patient and the therapist need to respect that defenses develop for a reason. Denial, like any other primary defense, must be approached gradually with full consideration for the needs of the patient. In cases where denial extends to issues of substance abuse, however, involvement in self-help groups for abstinence and recovery may need to be a mandatory addition to individual treatment.

Dissociation

This defense is a temporary alteration of the general integrative function of consciousness. Dissociative states range from momentary lapses of consciousness to severe episodes of fragmentation that include splitting, sleepwalking, psychogenic amnesia, derealization, depersonalization, and multiple personality disorder. Dissociation is a common neurotic defense. In its mildest form, it can be brought on to relieve temporarily stress and physical and psychological exhaustion. "Highway hypnosis" and intense daydreaming are common to most of us. Although these are distractions from present reality, they do not represent psychopathology.

In this section, I will review dissociation as a defense employed by adults who have experienced repeated trauma prior to maturity. Dissociation in this context is fragmenting and serves to detach the ego partially from painful memories and related affects. It is the extent to which the dissociative phenomenon disrupts functioning that determines pathology.

Dissociation may be induced with the onset of abuse and increase as the experiences of victimization are continuously repeated. For example, picture a child who is nurtured by her father, who over the years is the same person who engages in repeated sexual activity with her that continues throughout her childhood and adolescence. What enters into this picture is the development of intense ambivalence toward the abusive parent. Powerful feelings of love and hate develop toward the mother or other primary adult figures for their emotional unavailability or lack of protection. Unable either developmentally or physically to stop the abuse, the child's mind begins to escape what her body cannot through dissociation. This same mechanism of defense, which initially may serve the child as a protective shield against intolerable experiences, can take on pathogenic proportions later in development.

In some cases, dissociation can reduce the psychological pain stemming from repeated experiences of abuse or repress it entirely by what is known as psychogenic amnesia. In the more severe cases of abuse, the memories may become compartmentalized and maintained by split-off parts of the self, as is commonly noted in cases of multiple personality disorder. Unfortunately, repeated experiences of victimization do not remain dormant and tend to bring forth a myriad of negative symptoms such as nightmares, flooding, severe fragmentation, somatization, and depersonalization, which is often associated with parasuicidal behavior. The combination of these negative symptoms (particularly with concomitant substance abuse) can place the patient at a high risk for lethality. When the fragments of memory begin to break through the defensive barriers, self-doubt, self-blame, and a distorted perception of reality may be noted in the process of treatment. Over time, however, as the patient begins to verbalize and release recovered memories effectively, cohesion of self can begin, and the need for dissociation can be reduced.

Amnesia

Historically, amnesia was associated with hysteria, as observed by Freud and many of his colleagues. In present-day literature, the fact that amnesia is a common aftermath of trauma is well documented (Putnam 1985a, 1989b; van der Kolk 1987; Lowenstein 1990). In cases of post-traumatic amnesia, it is important to respect that such an extreme flight from the past may have either an integrative or fragmenting effect on the patient's ego. Trauma-related amnesia is a common finding in the lives of incest survivors. The level of psychopathology and suicide risk factors should be taken into account prior to the use of hypnosis or other memory-inducing techniques to break through the amnesic barriers. Decisions regarding the use of hypnoses should include a careful evaluation of ego strengths and deficits.

Psychogenic Fugue

Fugue states generally consist of a sudden departure away from home. When overwhelming memories or life events become unbearable, the patient may physically flee to another part of the country. In extreme cases of multiple personality disorder, the patient may begin life with a new identity. Fugue states are a severe form of dissociative disorder that can be profoundly disturbing for both the patient and the therapist.

A number of years ago a young woman, emotionally and psychologically impaired from the consequences of her sexual abuse, entered a psychotherapy group for incest survivors. One week, she neither called nor attended the group session. The following week, she came through the door with a cast on her leg and walking with a set of crutches. She later informed the group that she found herself in another state about six hours away from home. She had no recollection of her accident or how she had gotten to the hospital for treatment.

Many patients with a history of abuse and subsequent fugue states have been noted as having an excellent prognosis for recovery with the use of prolonged psychotherapy. Hypnosis and light intravenous barbiturate anesthesia may be useful to assist the patient to recover memories related to these episodes (Putnam 1989). A detailed history of the circumstances surrounding the various fugue episodes should be obtained by the therapist.

Sleepwalking

It has come to my attention that a number of patients with a history of sexual victimization have had experiences with sleepwalking. Although this behavior is more common in children and adolescents, Kales et al. (1980) found that psychopathology and difficulty in handling aggression were common in adults who had not outgrown the behavior of sleepwalking. Putnam (1989) identified a possible link between two of his patients with multiple personality disorder and somnambulistic wandering. To some extent, memories about the events that occur during episodes of sleepwalking are typically dissociated from consciousness. Accidents and injuries can happen during a sleepwalking episode.

Depersonalization/Derealization

Depersonalization is a dissociative experience that renders the self feeling estranged and unreal. When depersonalization experiences become persistent, leading to constant flight from internal reality, the risk of self-harm may be intensified. People with a history of sexual or physical victimization, concomitant psychopathology, and chemical dependency are at extreme risk during episodes of depersonalization. An example of depersonalization would be a patient who describes herself as feeling unreal and detached from the external world and from herself. These feelings are often transient and distort reality. Derealization is another defense with similar characteristics; in instances of derealization, external events and surroundings appear unreal and distorted. Both defenses are flights from reality and are image distorting. These defenses tend to surface when a patient is experiencing unwanted traumatic memories, feeling helpless, or overwhelmed by anxiety.

Depersonalization and derealization are common experiences in the lives of incest victims. They are also common findings in women who have a history of self-mutilating behavior. These types of dissociative experiences can arise instantaneously and impair normal functioning. It is important for the therapist to obtain a substantial history about the nature and extent of depersonalization and the role it plays in each dissociative patient's life. The emotional and psychological triggers should be noted when possible; establishing signals by reviewing the past episodes of depersonalization experiences allows both the patient and the therapist to identify the possible warning signs. I have found that trauma victims decrease the need for all dissociative phenomena as they increase their ability to cope with, understand, and verbalize the memories and emotions related to their history of abuse. The years of hidden cries and prolonged silence related to severe victimization, when faced in the context of psychotherapy, have the potential to free the mind from the constrictions of childhood trauma.

Splitting

For the purpose of defining it within the context of this chapter, splitting will be discussed as it serves to protect the ego through distortion and as defined by Kernberg (1980) as the active compartmentalization of contradictory experiences of the self and significant others. The defense of splitting may be similar to dissociative states in that both defenses are reality distorting and fragmenting. Splitting can be observed in the spectrum of neurotic to psychotic organization.

When a child is repeatedly victimized by a parent whom she was taught to trust and love, normal development cannot pursue its course. The self, the world, and those within it become either "all good" or "all bad." Trust, along with other necessary elements for normal development, is damaged. It is more than the history of victimization that leads to pathology; the therapist must include an understanding of the extent of dysfunction within the child's environment that leads to the pervasive use of primitive defenses, including splitting. The pathogenic use of splitting is exacerbated by the forced silence that often surrounds sexual victimization.

The adolescent or adult with a chronic history of incest, chaotic relationships, and an internalized sense of "badness" is often more susceptible to depression and suicide attempts. When an individual is unable to tolerate the feelings of shame and self-hatred, the internalized negative images are shifted by projecting them onto others. This continuously facilitates the cycle of splitting and other defensive operations. Clearly, an important component to the treatment is the interpretation of this defense and helping the patient understand the etiology of the disturbance. For the insightful patient, this often sheds new light on present behavior and diffuses, over time, the sense of shame and the need for splitting as a primary defense.

Minimizing

Minimizing is an image-distorting defense that leads to a distancing and detachment from thoughts and affects associated with trauma. When the psychological aftermath of trauma continues to invade the psyche unconsciously, defenses may begin to function maladaptively, and subsequent negative symptomotology will develop. Minimizing is a fairly common defense for the survivor of sexual abuse. Minimizing manifests as a partial detachment or splitting away from painful life events. This defense can seemingly dilute the experience of shame and guilt related to abuse, thus rendering their emotional impact less pronounced. In some cases, when minimizing is a primary defense, a history of long-standing abuse can be verbalized by the patient as though the story belonged to someone other than herself.

Minimizing is a stylistic way of coping with anxiety. Denial can be a precursor to minimizing and reaction formation. The distorting aspects of minimizing create a path for other defenses to come into play and push the traumatic memories further from awareness. Minimizing can also serve temporarily to conceal underlying rage and hostility toward significant others. When this defense continues into adulthood, it may mask the trauma but continue to play a significant role in the development of psychopathology. Through the use of minimizing, the ego can transiently deny the emotional impact of abuse and diminish anxiety.

The following clinical vignette illustrates the extent of impairment resulting from minimizing trauma: Shelly was a twenty-two-year-old woman who entered psychotherapy after a brief psychiatric hospitalization. In the initial phase of treatment, Shelly revealed a childhood history of emotional deprivation, abandonment, and neglect by her mother. She also experienced repeated sexual abuse throughout her childhood and adolescence. Despite the extent of her victimization, Shelly consistently remained isolated from the content and emotions of her traumatic childhood. Initially, she minimized the events of her childhood in terms of their impact on her state of depression or her fears of intimacy and attachment. She would have emotional outbursts at home, projecting her unresolved feelings of rage onto her boyfriend.

Shelly had been taught since childhood that painful emotions were not to be expressed and that deprivation was a part of life. At times, she learned to sublimate her pain through the use of school and other intellectual pursuits. Unable to complete her education, she used intellectualization, minimization, and denial to avoid having to cope with her sense of failure and shame. A considerable amount of time was spent in her treatment focusing on her history and both the adaptive and maladaptive use of minimization. After one year of psychotherapy, Shelly began to understand more about her use of minimization as a defense. Facing the horrors of the past, Shelly allowed herself to experience the sadness and tears that had remained beneath the surface for years. Both her fears and her desire for intimacy and self-awareness were evident in the context of psychotherapy and from the verbal reports pertaining to her relationships with significant others. Shelly's history of abuse and poor object relations since early childhood affected her ability to contain or neutralize powerful emotions and to develop mature significant relationships.

When the defense of minimizing remains untreated, it can manifest as a major resistance to the process of psychotherapy. The appearance of emotional numbing commonly seen in conjunction with minimizing can coexist with highly charged emotional outbursts. When attempting to resolve trauma-related pathology, it is important to explore the entire atmosphere surrounding the patient's past. The fear of experiencing traumatic memories and related emotions, masked by minimization, is far worse than the pain and mourning that leads to awareness and wholeness of self.

Projection

Projection is the attributing of thoughts or impulses that are unacceptable to oneself onto others and can lead to paranoid thinking. Projection can become pathological and increase paranoid ideation, thus facilitating the development of fixed delusions. Laughlin (1979) pointed out how psychotic projections, though sometimes bizarre and intriguing, are always tragic.

The case of Jacky is illustrative of Laughlin's perception. Jacky is a thirty-two-year-old single woman who is extremely bright and productive at work. She was raised in a dysfunctional family and was emotionally and sexually abused for many years by her father. As she matured, she feared her own sexuality and was terrified that a previous psychiatrist wanted to perform a clitoridectomy during one of her psychiatric hospitalizations. Jacky reported episodes of paranoid projection since adolescence. Although her delusions were often sophisticated and engaging, the extent of her pathology prevented her from completing law school. In some odd way, the web of paranoid projections appeared to provide both a continued sense of fear and comfort; the way in which she was able to engage others into the fabric of her delusions allowed her to maintain a feeling of intimacy that she could not achieve otherwise.

Vaillant (1977) pointed to the link between paranoid projection and the special intimacy that it provided with strangers. He noted that one can experience gratification from the thoughts of being sought after, especially when one does not feel loved. In Jacky's therapy, she is learning through the context of the therapeutic relationship that healthy intimacy and caring can be achieved without drama and projections. She is prepared for the clinical work to be slow and at times painful. It is quite conceivable that in cases like Jacky's, her psychopathology and use of projection are trauma induced.

Repression

Repression underlies the basis of all of the ego defenses. Repression is the process through which the ego rejects and avoids unwanted material from the conscious mind. This defense assigns the painful and intolerable data to the realm of the unconscious mind. Historically, the concept of repression has been related primarily to neurosis. Repression can range from being a higher-order defense to massive repression, a lower-order defense commonly noted in association with post-traumatic stress and psychotic reactions (Laughlin, 1979). It is the latter end of the continuum, the massive use of repression, that is clinically more problematic.

In cases of childhood incest, the long-term maintenance of secrecy and hidden silence related to the abuse facilitates repression. When disclosure of prolonged traumatic experiences leads to parental denial, it serves to compound the use of repression. When the abuse is severe and repeated, shame and guilt are internalized and directed at the self. This stimulates a split between self and others as either all good or all bad. In order to maintain a sense of goodness, even at the cost of developing a false self, the memories of the negative and intolerable abuse perpetrated by the parent or caretakers are repressed. As Miller (1984) writes, "Since the fact of abuse must be repressed for the sake of survival, all knowledge that would threaten to undo this repression must be warded off by every possible means, which ultimately results in an impoverishment of the personality and a loss of vital roots, manifested, for example in depression" (p. 160).

The following clinical vignette illustrates both the activation and release of the force of repression: Debbie was a thirty-one-year-old woman who entered treatment after a memory surfaced about her grandfather. When Debbie was in first grade, she had told her mother about being sexually abused. Her mother, who had a history of alcoholism, just cried; she was unable to offer Debbie any comfort or protection. Debbie never brought this matter to her mother again. The sexual abuse continued throughout Debbie's latency, but it was not until many years later (when Debbie joined a women's support group) that she had any memories of her childhood trauma. She began psychotherapy shortly after the abuse-related memories started to become conscious. Through the use of hypnosis, the previously repressed material continued to unfold and provided more details and missing links related to her past.

Somewhere between Debbie's latency and adulthood, she had completely repressed all memories of incest. Both emotional factors and life experiences influence repression. When Debbie entered treatment, she was depressed and overwhelmed; her defense of repression had become pathologically based. Although derepression was psychologically and emotionally painful, the abreaction and working through of previously repressed memories also provided psychic relief. (Abreaction is the discharge of repressed memories and affects related to trauma.)

Each patient will vary in his or her ability to contain the torment and anxiety brought about by breaking through the barriers of repression. The therapist can allow the patient to guide his or her own pace at derepression. Laughlin (1979) reminds us that "symptoms are often symbolic and disguised outward representations of various elements of unconscious conflicts, of which at least one aspect has been repressed" (p. 377). It is the abreacting and working through of the repressed material as it is brought to the awareness of the conscious mind that is often the most striking feature in working with adult survivors of incest.

Altruism

Altruism involves performing vicariously constructive services to others that also are gratifying to the self. Anna Freud (1980) delineates the defense of altruism as maintaining dual purposes. She describes the first purpose of altruism as providing an "interest in gratification of other people's instincts" as opposed to one's own (p. 129). She views the second purpose of altruism as serving to liberate inhibited activity and aggression as it relates to the self. Examples of altruistic behavior include public speaking, charitable services, and expressions of interest and empathy toward others. Altruism can temporarily reduce intrapsychic conflict and serve as an adaptive behavior for women recovering from the sequelae of sexual abuse.

A case example: Sally was a thirty-six-year-old divorced mother. She began psychotherapy after the disclosure of her daughter's sexual abuse at a local day care center. She also informed her therapist that she was sexually abused as a child and had never disclosed her story to anyone.

Initially, Sally was enraged about issues in her life related to victimization. Although Sally's anger seemed justified, the extent to which she experienced her rage was worrisome because of her desire to act out through the use of destructive behavior. Several weeks into therapy, Sally began to organize a project that involved the collection of toys for a child abuse clinic. To some extent, Sally gratified the aggressive impulses she felt toward the significant adults who betrayed her through her use of altruism. The positive responses she received for her charitable acts were comforting and provided relief from the intense feelings of pain, rage, and helplessness she had felt previously.

Humor

Playfulness and humor allows expression of emotions while reducing or eliminating stress and anxiety. For example, joke telling can be a vehicle for comic relief of forbidden or aggressive impulses. In this way, the use of humor can sometimes prevent destructive acting-out behavior. Humor is considered to be a mature defense that can assist in relieving tension and increase adaptivity (Perry and Cooper 1989; Valliant 1977).

In a weekly psychotherapy group for adult survivors of incest, the use of humor among members helped to create a safe holding environment. Like other defenses, however, when used in excess it also serves as a resistance to working on issues that would induce painful memories. The goal is not to eliminate the element of humor. Interpretation of the function of humor within the context of group, though, helped move the patients to a more insightful position that eventually allowed for the containment of painful affects and related memories.

For those women whose lives are filled with painful abuse related memories, humor is a blessing. Overall, humor may provide relief from stressful situations and facilitate the promotion of psychological health. The ability to express humor in the context of psychotherapy may enhance the prognosis and prove to be a curative element in the treatment process. An adult patient with a diagnosis of multiple personality disorder and severe history of satanic cult abuse talked about the use of humor in her life. She said, "Laughter is the best medicine, even if I'm not really happy."

There is a need for further research on interrelationships between humor, psychological health, and psychotherapy. Clinical studies reporting on the use of humor among trauma survivors could produce new insights for psychotherapists. Many of us in the field of trauma are already aware of the ways in which humor reduces the stress inherent in our clinical work.

Sublimation

Sublimation is the unconscious process of rechanneling aggressive or sexual impulses into culturally acceptable vehicles for expression. For example, the desire for a married woman to have an affair may be transformed into writing a novel, poetry, or some other creative project. Another example of sublimation is diverting unacceptable aggressive feelings about someone by becoming involved with competitive sports, aerobic exercises, or martial arts. The rewards of sublimation often include personal gratification or acknowledgement from others.

I have found the use of artwork, poetry, letter writing, and journal keeping to be extremely useful in the treatment of women with a childhood history of incest and satanic cult abuse. The use of aerobic exercises and sports can reduce anxiety and, in some cases, help to slow down or divert the experience of flooding related to intrusive traumatic memories.

In cases of severe and repeated sexual abuse and related environmental stress, repetition of impaired defensive styles will be noted. Early childhood trauma may have a profound affect upon the development of mature defenses that could assist with sublimation, frustration tolerance, and impulse control. In adulthood, the inability to rely on mature defenses can increase the extent of acting-out and behavioral reenactment.

Many women who have survived sexual trauma have talked about feeling empowered by learning martial arts. A common symptom seen in patients with a history of childhood trauma is learned helplessness. Through the use of sublimation a sense of accomplishment and feeling of control can be established. This may reduce internalized experiences stemming from childhood trauma where the victimization was not in the patients control and where she was helpless to stop the abuse.

Supporting creative expression in victimized patients can prove to be an extremely enlightening experience for both the patient and the therapist.

Suppression

Suppression is the conscious or semiconscious decision to defer focusing on unpleasant subject matter. This means that one delays—

not avoids—dealing with unpleasant memories, situations, or feelings.

A case example: Ms. Topin is a young woman presently in medical school. Two weeks prior to entering psychotherapy, she was raped by a masked man who had entered her home in the middle of the night. Knowing that she had an important exam, she engaged the support of her mother and dealt with the police, but postponed entering psychotherapy. Once she began treatment, she was psychologically able to focus on her emotions and fears related to the rape. Ms. Topin was able to suppress the rape incident sufficiently to complete her exam successfully. Fortunately, she also realized that she would benefit psychologically from clinical intervention.

Sgroi (1982) wrote about the suppression phase that often follows disclosure of child sexual abuse. Sgroi's concern was that the suppression of the abuse experience commonly noted in victims of incest and their families could foster denial if the environment rejected the allegations of abuse. The sexually abused child needs support and a safe environment to express feelings and thoughts related to the experiences of sexual abuse in order to continue toward healthy development.

As adults, the unmet emotional and psychological needs related to years of abuse and subsequently suppressed can take shape by allowing the therapist to provide the safety and nurturance that the abusive parent was not able to supply.

Summary

Understanding ego defenses and their role in adaptation and psychopathology creates an important foundation for the process of psychotherapy. Learning to observe defenses can provide insight, allowing previously unconscious psychic operations to surface into awareness. In this way, psychotherapy becomes a vehicle for self-reflection and acceptance of previously denied or repressed material. In time, as trust and safety develop in therapy, defensive resistance will be reduced. The therapist should always respect the patient's need for the use of specific defenses and not stimulate decompensation by intervening with interpretation of defenses too early in treatment.

Interpreting the nature of defenses is made clearer and more tolerable when understood in the context of their possible development and protective functions. The therapist must be careful to remain empathic and not to induce further shame, thus creating a safe holding environment for the disclosure of the deep-rooted pain related to victimization previously masked by complex layers of defenses.

This chapter is meant to serve as a guide to consider the implication of defenses in the treatment of victimization and psychopathology. Further research is needed about the intrapsychic development of ego defenses subsequent to trauma. A comprehensive study of defense mechanisms would reveal the complex layers of defensive operations used to ward off unbearable realities.

Children are neither psychologically or developmentally able to mitigate cruel and repeated forms of traumatic abuse. Initially, defenses serve to protect children from intolerable situations and experiences. In adulthood, the same defensive structure designed for protection can become pathogenic. Respect must be given to understanding the nature of the patient's defensive profile as seen in the context of psychotherapy.

Clarification of defensive operations can serve to define the therapeutic tasks for a corrective emotional experience. Healing from the deleterious effects of childhood victimization takes time and effort, often for both the therapist and the patient. In cases where psychopathology prevails, long term psychotherapy is recommended to overcome resistance and work toward the establishment of emotional health and maturity.

References

Blum, H. (1987). The role of identification in the resolution of trauma (Anna Freud Memorial Lecture). *Psychoanalytic Quarterly* 56:609–627.

Burgess, A. W., and Holmstrom, L. (1978). Accessory to sex: pressure, sex, and secrecy. In Burgess, A. W., Groth, A., Holmstrom, L. L., and Sgroi, S. (Ed.). *Sexual Assault of Children and Adolescents,* Lexington, MA: Lexington Books.

Cloninger, C. R., and Guze, S. B. (1970). Female criminals: their personal, familial, and social backgrounds: the relation of these to the diagnosis of sociopathy and hysteria. *Archives of General Psychiatry* 23:554–558.

de Young, M. (1982). Self-injurious behavior in incest victims: a research note. *Child Welfare* 61:577–584.

Finkelhor, D. and Brown, A. (1985). The traumatic impact of child sexual abuse: a conceptualization. *American Journal of Orthopsychiatry 55* (4):530–541.

Freud, A. (1980) *The Ego and the Mechanisms of Defense,* New York: International Universities Press, Inc.

Freud, S. (1958). Remembering, repeating and working through. In J. Stachey (Ed. & Trans.) *The Standard Edition of the Complete Psychological Works of Sigmund Freud, Vol. 12,* (Original work published in 1914.)

Goodwin, J. (1990). Applying to adult incest victims what we have learned from victimized children. In Kluft, R. P. (Ed.), *Incest Related Syndromes of Adult Psychopathology.* Washington, DC. American Psychiatric Press pp. 55–74.

Goodwin, J., Simms, M. and Bergman, R. (1979) Hysterical seizures: a sequel to incest. *American Journal of Orthopsychiatry 49:698–703.*

Green, A. H. (1978). Psychopathology of Abused Children. *Journal of the American Academy of Child Psychiatry 17:356–371.*

Kales, A., Soldatos, C. R., Caldwell, A. B., Kales, J. D., Humphrey, F. J., Charney, D. S., and Schweitzen, P. K. (1980). Somnambulism. *Archives of General Psychiatry 37:*1406–1410.

Kernberg, O. (1980) *Internal World and External Reality: Object Relations Theory Applied.* New York: Jason Aronson.

Laughlin, H. P. (1979). *The Ego and its Defenses.* New York: Jason Aronson.

Lewis, W. C., and Berman M. (1965). Studies of conversion hysteria. *Archives of General Psychiatry 13:275–282.*

Lowenstein, R. J. (1990). Somatoform disorders in victims of incest and child abuse. In Kluft, R. P. (Ed.), *Incest Related Syndromes of Adult Psychopathology.* Washington DC.: American Psychiatric Press, pp. 75–107.

Maltz, W., and Holman, B. (1987). *Incest and Sexuality: A Guide to Understanding and Healing.* Massachusetts: Lexington Books.

Miller, A. (1984). *Thou Shalt Not Be Aware: Society's Betrayal of the Child.* New York: Farrar, Straus, Giroux.

Perry, C. J., and Cooper, H. S. (1989). An empirical study of defense mechanisms. *Archives of General Psychiatry 64:444–452.*

Putnam, F. W. (1985). Dissociation: a response to extreme trauma. In Kluft, R. P. (Ed.), *The Childhood Antecedents of Multiple Personality,* Washington, DC: American Psychiatric Press.

Putnam, F. W. (1989). *Diagnosis and Treatment of Multiple Personality Disorder.* New York: Guildford Press.

Russell, D. E. H. (1986). *The Secret Trauma: Incest in the Lives of Girls and Women.* New York: Basic Books.

Sgroi, S. M. (ed.). (1982). *Handbook of Clinical Intervention in Child Sexual Abuse,* Lexington, MA: D.C. Heath.

Shapiro, S. (1987). Self-mutilation and self-blame in incest victims. *American Journal of Psychotherapy* 41:46–55.

Shapiro, S. and Dominiak, G. (1990). Common psychological defenses seen in the treatment of sexually abused adolescents, *American Journal of Psychotherapy* 44:68–74.

Stone, M. H. (1990). Incest in the borderline patient. In Kluft, R. P. (Ed.), *Incest Related Syndromes of Adult Psychopathology.* Washington, DC. American Psychiatric Press. 183–204.

Vailliant, G. (1977). *Adaptation to Life.* Boston, MA. Little, Brown and Company.

van der Kolk, B. A. (1989). Compulsion to repeat the trauma. In Kluft, R. P. (Ed.), *The Psychiatric Clinics of North America.* Philadelphia. W. B. Saunders Co. 12:2:389–408.

van der Kolk, B. A. (1987). *Psychological Trauma.* Washington, DC. American Psychiatric Press.

4

Hypnotic Constructions of Reality in Trauma and Treatment

Elizabeth P. Hess

Johanna notes in therapy that she always drives well below the speed limit, but still becomes anxious each time she sees a police car. She has an overwhelming fear that the police will stop her, arrest her, and take her to jail. She gains insight in treatment that her fear is based on dread that the police will discover behaviors that she was forced to perform as a child victimized by a cult. Nonetheless, some of her nervousness while driving persists.

Susan is enjoying dinner in a Mexican restaurant with a friend. She happens to glance up and sees a piñata shaped like a horse decorating one of the rafters. Immediately, a panic attack ensues. Several weeks later in therapy, she uncovers a childhood memory of being raped in a garage where an old rocking horse was stored in the rafters. She had focused on the rocking horse in an effort to minimize her awareness of the rape.

Ann has worked hard in therapy to gain the strength necessary to go through with a divorce. She comes very upset to the first session after going to court for the divorce. She states that she cannot remember anything that happened between going up the steps to the courthouse and leaving the building later with her lawyer, who assured her that nothing else remained to be done to complete the divorce.

Bethany is a research subject in the standardization sample of Hilgard's work at Stanford University to develop a hypnotic susceptibility scale. While in a hypnotic trance, she is told she can no longer smell. The researcher then asks her to inhale with a bottle of ammonia placed under her nose. She is disappointed at smelling the ammonia quite clearly, and assumes that she is not a good hypnotic subject. The researcher then tells her that she is able to smell again, and again asks her to inhale. She inhales as vigorously as before and is startled by overwhelming ammonia fumes that cause her nose and eyes to water. She has been unaware of how well the hypnotic suggestions have been working.

The first two case examples above show typical experiences and feelings reported by survivors of severe trauma in the process of their treatment. The third case shows an isolated incidence of amnesia during a highly stressful incident. The fourth is drawn from the author's personal experience as a naive hypnotic subject in the 1960s. Although the first three are examples of dissociation and the last is an example of hypnosis, they share in common the mind's capacity to alter its construction of perceived reality. This capacity can be useful, as in a hypnotic induction to block perceptions of pain. It can be a relatively harmless defense mechanism, as for Ann, who was shielded from direct memory of the details of court proceedings in her divorce. Or it can be a highly disrupting disorder in which a person is locked into perceiving present reality again and again as being as equally dangerous and shaming as past traumatic experiences have been. In each case, the perception of reality has been altered. And, in each case, the person's own awareness of the degree to which his or her mind has performed this alteration is only partial.

Persons suffering from severe trauma almost always experience some dissociative symptoms similar to those described above, particularly if the trauma is prolonged and inescapable (Terr 1991). Since hypnosis and dissociation use the same mental processes, hypnosis can be a powerful tool to help patients explore and change their altered perceptions of reality. Even if formal hypnosis is not used in treatment, however, therapists need to understand the hypnotic qualities of dissociation in order to conceptualize their patient's symptoms clearly and to facilitate change.

The Structure of Hypnopathology

A thorough description of the interrelation between hypnosis and dissociation is provided by Bliss (1986). He and others have formulated several models of the mechanisms through which the mind reacts in the face of either hypnosis or trauma. In both circumstances, the mind enters an altered state of consciousness not accessible in the normal state. Tinnin (1990) draws on MacLean's (1973) organizational structure of the brain, in which the most primitive "reptilian" component mediates consciousness at the level of physical sensation.

This component is located physiologically in the brain stem and reticular system. The next highest component "paleomammalian" mediates via emotions and corresponds with the midbrain and limbic system. Finally, the neocortex the "neomammalian" component has the capacity for intellectual functioning, including concepts of time, relative comparison, and language. Simultaneously, Tinnin (1990) postulates a dominant "governing mental system" (p. 155), located in the dominant left cerebral hemisphere of the brain, that mediates conscious perception of reality and the self from approximately age three on.

Both Tinnin (1990) and Fish-Murray, Koby, and van der Kolk (1987) theorize that in the face of trauma, consciousness is no longer mediated by the normal, mature left dominant cerebral cortex, but that regression occurs to more primitive areas (either right hemisphere and/or reptilian and paleomammalian levels). Trauma experienced in this way is then cut off from the person's normal mode of being, in which the person functions out of the more mature level of the brain. Essentially state-dependent "learning" of the event occurs that will only become accessible again if a similar state is induced in the patient. The traumatic material remains unconscious, or in more severe cases with repeated trauma, the alternate mode of consciousness may develop into a more active force, leaving the patient with two or more perceptions of reality with little or no interconnection. This can result in multiple personality disorder.

Material thus trapped in the unconscious portion of the mind is harmful not only because it leaves the person vulnerable to flashbacks, intrusive nightmares, and so forth, but also because the more primitive component of the mind lacks needed capabilities for working through this material and placing it in context. It is as if the person facing this material is perpetually limited to confronting it as a powerless, very young child with no consciousness that good events also occur, that he or she is not bad or to blame for what has occurred, or that the trauma will come to an end.

The following example illustrates this dilemma: An accomplished professional, well-known for his caring treatment for those seeking his services, works extensive hours. His doctor has instructed him to reduce his work load for health reasons. He feels that he cannot, because time off is "not productive." He readily admits to his therapist that he would encourage a colleague in the same circumstances to slow down and be less self-demanding, but feels inexplicably that he cannot give himself the same consideration. Exploration of childhood history gradually reveals prolonged abuse, with constant parental accusations of being "good for nothing." Until experiences from childhood causing feelings of shame and failure are worked through, the patient's mature, intellectual understanding is ineffective in helping him.

A parallel process occurs with hypnosis. By means of hypnotic induction, the subject shifts into an altered state of consciousness in which normal intellectual functioning is suspended in favor of a more regressed state in which many critical faculties are diminished and active volition is exchanged for a much more passive stance. In this state, the subject allows the hypnotist, via suggestion, to alter the subject's perceptions of reality. This occurs through highly selected focusing of attention, so that certain facets of the person's external and/or internal perception of self and the world are highlighted or obscured. By using hypnosis, a therapist can help the patient to reenter the altered, regressed state in which trauma occurred and to reintegrate this material into his or her normal conscious state. In addition, hypnosis allows the artificial quality of reentering the past state to be greatly diminished, so that the necessary emotional engagement with the material can occur for changed perceptions and new insight to become "real" for the patient. Gruenewald (1984) values this quality of hypnosis, in which internal reworking and remembering takes on the impact of reality, as an important key to facilitate change. She compares it to the play or other role-playing qualities in treatment that allow transference to be an effective tool in psychodynamic psychotherapy.

In actual clinical practice, the statements and attitudes of the therapist often take on the weight of hypnotic suggestion for trauma survivors, even without formal hypnotic trance induction. Because of the transference qualities of the therapeutic relationship, patients often regress into a somewhat passive, receptive mode while in the therapy session, which allows this phenomenon to occur. Furthermore, trauma survivors with marked dissociative features are demonstrably excellent hypnotic subjects, because they have learned to employ self-hypnosis as a defense against trauma. Such highly hypnotizable persons can be quite susceptible to suggestion, even in a normal level of consciousness, presumably because of more ready access (on average) to the altered state of consciousness in which hypnosis occurs.

If the therapist is aware of this trait in trauma survivors, it can be used to advantage to guide the patient continually toward a more empowering conception of reality. If the therapist is unaware of this factor or intimidated by the patient's pathology, however, unfortunate results can occur. For example, trauma survivors almost inevitably express at some point in treatment the sense that their rage is so great that they feel they will explode into destructive behavior. Their self-perception will be greatly different with a therapist who calmly normalizes the situation, commenting that most trauma survivors feel this and that acting on the feelings is neither necessary nor inevitable, compared to a therapist who projects a sense of panic and fear that the patient will lose control. The second therapist is inadvertently suggesting to the more primitive, unconscious aspect of the patient that the world is an uncertain, out-of-control, and dangerous place, and that the patient is a bad person who will do awful things. Specific ways to use hypnotherapeutic interventions to help trauma survivors will be discussed later.

Symptoms Resulting from Hypnotic Phenomena in Dissociation

Changes in perception that can occur in both hypnosis and dissociation are profound and far-reaching. Furthermore, these changes in perception can have a real effect on physiological functioning. For example, a hypnotic subject given a block of wood and told it is a hot piece of iron may have his or her skin redden as the mind "believes" that it has been burnt. An opposite hypnotic effect occurs where surgery is possible, without anesthesia and with little bleeding, when the patient is given the suggestion that the affected body part is made of plastic and is no longer part of his or her body.

Bliss (1986) provides a helpful listing of the various types of perceptual alteration that can occur in dissociative and/or hypnotic states. First, changes can occur in *motor functions*. For example, a person may find himself partially or fully paralyzed; this might occur as he is beginning to retrieve memories of abuse in which he was tied and unable to move. Using MacLean's model, this memory is accessible only at the level of physical sensation (the reptilian level), resulting in his body reenacting its state of being immovable but with no cognitive understanding of the surrounding circumstances. Similarly, changes can occur in *sensation*. The same patient might have numbness in his hands or feet as his reptilian level of consciousness remembers numbness occurring when blood flow was constricted by the ropes tying him.

Frequently, changes in *mood and affect* occur, as with the earlier example of Susan's panic attack at seeing the pinata. The figure of the horse serves as a conditioned stimulus that brings back the paleomammalian (or emotional) level of consciousness that became present when she was raped. Again, she has no intellectual insight into the source of her panic, but is only aware of the feeling itself. Corresponding changes in *autonomic processes* can occur as a trauma survivor struggles with unintegrated levels of consciousness. These changes can include changes in blood pressure, raised or lowered body temperature, clinical shock, nausea, and so on. Other hypnotic phenomena that occur in dissociation include changes in *perception of time*; frank distortion of *memory,* such as the creation of screen memories to block the survivor's awareness of an even more disturbing factual memory; distortion of memory in the form of amnesia for specific periods or time or events; and changes in *cognition,* such as gaining or losing the capacity to speak a second language.

Not all of these changes are negative, especially at the time of the trauma. Trauma survivors may well have learned to block out emotion, pain, or fatigue in order to survive. Also, the blocking of memory that occurs due to the dissociation of different levels of consciousness serves the survivor well to prevent becoming completely overwhelmed by repeated or prolonged trauma. In a similar fashion, by retreating to a more primitive level of consciousness in which abstract intellectual processes are not possible, the patient escapes knowledge of the clear probability that abuse will occur again in the future. Finally, in the case of psychic betrayal (such as incest), the patient may have retreated to a primitive level of moral judgment in which he or she may be able to believe that he or she is totally to blame for the abuse, thus preserving an ideal image of the perpetrator as a good, nonbetraying adult. This allows a perception of the world as a fair, predictable environment in which the patient can have a sense of control, even though an enormous personal price is extracted in shame and loss of self-worth.

Trauma survivors presenting for treatment show characteristic symptoms as a consequence of dissociation. Often, somatic reenactment of the trauma is present, with no insight as to the cause. These "body memories" seem to represent the mind's effort to somehow move this material to a higher level of consciousness so that the material can be integrated. By producing pain or discomfort, a signal is given that a problem is present that needs to be resolved.

A second hallmark symptom of trauma survivors is the intermittent presence of immature logic. As noted above, they tend to suffer from unreasonable shame and self-blame. In addition, they greatly underestimate their own power to resolve problems in their present environment, as if trapped in the perceptual world of a helpless small child. Also, their sense of proportion and perspective is distorted, as if they are not yet capable of making reasonable comparisons from one situation to another. Caroline Fish-Murray et al. (1987) point out that these are cognitive states typical of children who have not yet reached the Piagetian formal-operations level of development; or even, at times, the concrete-operations level. This immature logic can occur either because the trauma took place when the child was very young, or because of regression to a more immature state of consciousness in the face of trauma occurring at a later age.

A third symptom that trauma survivors present is marked disruption in memory and concentration. Frequently, they will be unable to recall large portions of their childhood or of later periods in which abuse occurred. In addition, they have difficulty focusing consistently in the present. This disrupted attention appears to occur as a result of the unintegrated levels of consciousness within their minds, so that their higher-level conscious reasoning is always at risk of being distracted by the more primitive, dissociated state of consciousness.

A fourth symptom is the loss of flexibility and control over the use of dissociation as a protective defense. At times, a survivor can describe early efforts to take themselves deliberately away from conscious awareness of traumatic event. For trauma survivors exposed to repeated or prolonged stress, however, the dissociative reaction becomes an involuntary, conditioned reflex that occurs in the presence of even mild stress (Terr 1991). For example, a patient may find herself totally unable to recall information given her over the phone. As soon as she starts a phone conversation, she experiences worry that she might not remember the call accurately or might have to ask the caller to repeat information. This worry produces sufficient stress to trigger total dissociation for the content of any call, no matter how benign.

A final symptom is that these survivors live in a self-constructed reality in which they perceive themselves only as victims. They approach life almost totally defensively and fail to use sources of power available to them to improve their situation, either within their own repertoire of skills and assets or in cooperation with those who could assist them in their environment. Part of the reason for this is that their dissociative defense preempts any more active problem-solving strategy. In the face of a problem or stress, they tend to be thrown into an altered state of consciousness that is more primitive and lacks a capacity for adequate insight and planning. Although this may buffer them to some extent from the full emotional impact of their present stress, it also makes them extremely vulnerable to re-victimization.

Hypnotic Conceptualization in Assessment of Trauma Survivors

When assessing a trauma survivor entering psychotherapy, therapists will find it helpful to probe the nature of any dissociative symptoms that are present. These can vary considerably. Terr (1991), for example, finds that children suffering from one single traumatic event are more likely to experience what she calls a Type I trauma disorder, with full, detailed memory of the traumatic event; a tendency to re-work the incident cognitively in order to find an explanation as to why it occurred; and misperceptions subsequent to the trauma, including visual hallucinations, misidentifications, and/or time distortions. In contrast, Terr finds children suffering from prolonged or repeated trauma to experience a Type II trauma disorder, in which they display massive denial, repression, dissociation, self-anesthesia, self-hypnosis, identification with the aggressor, and aggression turned against the self. At times, both types of trauma can occur in the same individual. These symptoms often persist into adulthood; a careful inventory of presenting symptoms is important in formulating a safe and effective treatment plan and may also give clues as to the nature of trauma that has not yet been consciously remembered.

Because dissociative symptoms are such an automatic part of trauma patients' perceptual systems, they may not volunteer information about them or be aware that they represent a problem. For example, one patient entering treatment in her thirties was highly surprised to hear from her therapist that most people can remember major life events that occurred before age twelve. Another adolescent patient was cutting her arms in a dissociated state prior to treatment.

Although she was vaguely aware that the wounds existed (and wore long sleeves to hide them), she had no concern about them until her mother happened to see her arms bleeding one day and brought her for treatment. Careful assessment can help to draw out important treatment information with such patients. The Dissociative Experiences Questionnaire (Bernstein and Putnam 1986) is one structured interview instrument designed to screen for these symptoms. In addition, several areas of important inquiry are described below, with suggestions as to possible questions that may prove helpful in eliciting symptoms.

Depersonalization is often present for trauma survivors, either intermittently or as an almost steady state. Asking the patient, "Do you feel unreal at times?" may elicit information in this area. In addition, it is wise throughout treatment to be alert to statements that may be uttered as a passing side comment, such as "I feel like I just got here," or "I feel like my head just went into a fog."

Regression is a common problem for trauma patients. Under stress, they find themselves functioning out of a self-perception from a much younger age. Even the stress of a therapy intake interview may cause this phenomenon to occur. A patient who has been calmly answering questions and describing past trauma may rather abruptly become tearful or angry, use a much more primitive vocabulary, and/or react to the therapist as a person who is likely to punish or belittle the patient. A loss of previously noted capacity for logic and/or perspective may be noted. For example, a patient may begin describing incest events with a sense of anger at the perpetrator, but then suddenly express extreme guilt and shame at being involved in such an act. Questions that can clarify the presence of regression include asking, "How old do you feel right now?" or "How old did you feel when your boss confronted you and you had to run from the room?"

At times, the patient may be unable to examine her or his feeling state in terms of chronological age, especially if material surfacing has been stored in a more primitive level of consciousness. A technique that can help to some extent is to ask the patient to picture herself or himself in the situation being examined (such as a confrontation with a boss) and then ask, "How tall do you feel? How tall does the boss feel?" Patients may be surprised to realize that they have pictured themselves as only child-sized in relation to a very large-appearing boss. (Note that asking the patient to picture the scene vividly may put many patients into a light hypnotic trance, because of their high susceptibility to suggestion. Choices about using or not using hypnosis will be discussed further below.)

Amnesia always requires careful assessment, for the obvious reason that it is very difficult to remember that one has forgotten something. Until the patient or someone else attempts to retrieve memories about a particular event, it is impossible to realize that the memory is missing. Questions should be asked about what the patient recalls of early childhood, elementary school years, adolescence, and so forth. It can be fruitful to explore if memories for events in the home are more clear or less clear than memories for events at school or in the community. Although there are inevitable exceptions, areas in which amnesia is present are likely to contain traumatic material that has been dissociated or repressed. In addition, it is important to assess the extent to which amnesia continues to occur in the present. For example, if a patient is describing an argument with a spouse, it is wise to ask, "Do you remember what you said (or felt, or did) in that argument?" What appears to be simple reticence, or summarizing an incident in order to save time, may actually be amnesia of which the patient is either fully or partially unaware.

One particular instance of amnesia that can be very frustrating, but needs to be acknowledged by both the therapist and patient, occurs when the patient is unable to remember what has happened in the previous therapy session. This may occur when a session has been too emotionally overwhelming for the patient, causing a dissociative reaction. Often, if the therapist gives a reminder of the key content of the session, the patient is then able to retrieve the memory into consciousness. Therapists may find it routinely useful to begin the next session after a difficult one with, "What do you remember from our last time together?"

Analgesia is a useful dissociative defense when confronted with inescapable pain. As in other areas, inquires need to be made into instances of analgesia occurring both in the past and in the present. For example, one might ask, "What was the pain like when your father hit you?" or "What do you feel when you cut yourself?"

Intrusive phenomena can take a variety of forms. A patient may have repetitive dreams with themes or content related to past trauma. Frequently, trauma survivors may experience paranoidlike phenomena without psychosis. They may describe fears that people can tell just by looking at them that they have been abused, or that people are following them when they go down the street. Many find it impossible to sleep at night unless the room has a light so that any danger can be seen. Another form of intrusive experience involves sensory hallucinations; a patient may complain of tasting blood or other unpleasant flavors, or of smelling burning flesh. Auditory and visual hallucinations are common. Finally, full-blown flashbacks can occur in which the patient reexperiences aspects of trauma that had been previously encapsulated in a different level of consciousness via dissociation. These flashbacks may range from brief glimpses of sometimes minor details from the traumatic event to entire scenes. Patients describe these flashbacks as extremely vivid, as if they were actually reliving the event. Often, patients are fearful to report intrusive phenomena for fear of being labeled as crazy. Giving reassurance that such experiences are a common consequence of trauma can help normalize their experience for them.

Consciously employed dissociative strategies often coexist with unconscious symptoms in trauma survivors. It is important to identify these strategies. First of all, they can be very effective coping mechanisms that should not be eliminated until the patient has available a better means of dealing with stressful feelings and situations. Secondly, when one points out to patients their capacity to choose a helpful dissociative strategy, they begin to change their self-concept from one of totally passive victims to active agents capable of making useful choices in their lives. To assess the presence of such strategies, questions can be asked concerning any images the patient uses to help calm down or go to sleep; ways the patient shuts out of awareness aspects of the environment that are displeasing or overwhelming; ways the patient helps himself or herself feel more safe in the therapy session; and so forth.

Finally, *encapsulated affective or cognitive states* need to be assessed. Any evidence of splitting should be noted. In addition, many patients may make statements such as, "There's a part of me that's totally competent, but there's another part that just wants to die." Due to the recent popularity of ego state therapy (Watkins and Watkins, 1979) and various forms of "inner child" work, many patients may refer to a child and other parts within that are frightened, ashamed, or angry. In addition to understanding the patient's perception of divisions within the self, it is important to determine the degree of permeability between these various self states. If total or near total impermeability exists—with parts taking over conscious control of the patient, amnesic barriers between parts, and/or significant influence asserted over the patient's actions and feelings by unconscious parts—a diagnosis of multiple personality disorder needs to be seriously considered.

In all of these areas of assessment, the underlying issue is the patient's altered perceptions of reality, both in terms of faulty access to the past and in terms of disrupted perception of the present. What began as a helpful self-hypnotic mechanism for dealing with trauma has become a rigid, involuntary defense that divides the patient off from necessary self-knowledge concerning history, feelings, and interpersonal relationships. Mapping out the extent and nature of this defense is an important step to effective treatment.

Hypnotically Based Treatment Interventions

Because survivors of trauma suffer from unintegrated states of consciousness, problems arise in treatment that do not occur with nondissociative patients. Spiegel (1990) and Tinnin (1990) both give excellent analyses of the difference between dissociation and repression. In a nondissociative patient, information may be recovered that has been repressed; however, only the specific painful or conflicting content involved has been repressed. In dissociation, an entire state of consciousness has been created and submerged below the normal state of awareness, with its own distinctly primitive perceptions and cognitive style.

In cases of dissociation, a patient frequently will present for treatment with a sense that trauma has occurred, but both the therapist and the patient will have great difficulty accessing this dissociated material for working through. In some instances, this takes the form of having factual recall for the trauma, but no access to the more primitive affective dimensions. In other instances, more primitive aspects from the patient's dissociated level of consciousness are present, but with a substantial barrier between somatic or emotional memories and the verbal level of factual memory in which integration and mastery can occur. This can lead at times to the patient becoming overwhelmed by primitive material breaking through into normal consciousness, with the affective impact as if the trauma were occurring in the present. In this situation, the patient can become so flooded that it is difficult to maintain awareness of the normal state of consciousness at all. The patient is likely to feel disoriented and out of control.

Since self-hypnosis is the mechanism through which dissociation occurs, the process of therapy with dissociative patients inevitably involves hypnotic facets, even if the therapist would prefer otherwise. Ubiquitous trance states are a given with these patients. As noted above, trauma survivors frequently enter a spontaneous trance, and this is especially likely in therapy sessions in which past trauma is the focus. These dissociative trances may not be obvious to the patient or to the therapist, unless the therapist is alert to their presence. Furthermore, trauma can only be worked through by accessing the level of consciousness where the perception and memory of the trauma is experienced and stored. This requires engaging in a hypnoticlike process that allows shifting back and forth between the various levels of consciousness. Only in the end stage of this process, when the experiences are fully integrated, can therapy proceed in a trance-free mode, with mature logic and perception brought fully to bear. Before this, the typical course of therapy will go back and forth between levels of consciousness, like archaeologists going down into earlier levels in the earth and bringing up artifacts to the surface to be examined in the light of day.

Therapeutic integration of dissociated consciousness can occur with or without the use of formal hypnosis, but the process is always hypnotic, regardless. How should a therapist decide when a formal hypnotic induction is indicated?

When the therapeutic process includes overtly labeled, formal hypnotic inductions and trances, several factors come into play. The patient may well benefit from the sense of structure and control attributed to being hypnotized by a trusted hypnotherapist. Though the patient may fear loss of control in confronting material when using his or her own dissociative techniques, a formal hypnotic induction gives the clear message that the therapist is in charge of the process and will see to it that safe and productive work occurs. The negative aspect of this same factor is that the patient may have great difficulty giving over control to the therapist because of trust issues stemming from being abused. This is especially difficult if the abusers themselves used hypnosis as part of the abuse process. Educating the patient, however, about his or her dissociative defenses as being similar to hypnotic states can reinforce the therapeutic alliance.

A second factor that can be very beneficial is that hypnosis provides an opportunity for relating to material in an "as if" state, without the patient having to commit himself or herself fully to what ensues during hypnosis. For example, hypnosis gives patients permission to try a new way of perceiving or being without having to give up old patterns entirely. They can experience feelings such as anger or fear, or allow themselves a new degree of vulnerability, without giving up a "normal" surface stance of placidity or reserve. After experiencing these new ways of being under hypnosis, the patient is likely to find it easier to choose to maintain these changes in the normal conscious state. In the same fashion, hypnosis gives a patient permission to regress intentionally in order to deal with traumatic material while assuring that he or she will return to normal on leaving the trance state. A final factor in favor of using formal hypnosis is the clear message to the patient that the hypnotic ability that has been wreaking havoc, with the patient having little or no sense of conscious control during dissociation, can be brought under control and become a matter of choice.

A more informal approach, making use of the natural suggestibility of the patient and avoiding formal hypnotic inductions, produces a different set of factors to consider. On the positive side, these informal suggestions form part of the natural, ongoing therapeutic relationship. Insights and change that occur may be more easily integrated into daily life. Furthermore, the patient is more empowered, seeing herself or himself as the change agent rather than submitting passively to the hypnotic treatment administered by the therapist. Finally, therapists with little or no training in clinical hypnosis can have this approach available to them, as no overt expectations are raised concerning trance inductions, the power of suggestions, and so on.

An obvious drawback to this approach is that the therapist does not have the option of using hypnotic trances in order to reach levels of consciousness otherwise unavailable, or of providing explicit suggestions that can help with management of dissociative symptoms. Any therapist working with trauma survivors will find training in clinical hypnosis extremely helpful, so that she or he can become thoroughly familiar with hypnotic phenomena and be aware of these when they occur in treatment. Definitely, no therapist should attempt formal hypnotic treatment without direct training by a qualified, experienced hypnotherapist and ongoing supervision until hypnotic skills are mastered.

Either approach (or both combined) will allow the therapist to help the patient gradually to give up dysfunctional self-hypnotic techniques and to develop more self-aware, effective ways of functioning.

This process needs to proceed slowly, as dissociation has been the patient's main defense. At first, minor shifts can be encouraged toward more benign options within the dissociative continuum. For example, a person who experiences severe abdominal pain as the somatic memory of past abuse can be guided to use a milder somatic symptom instead, such as numbness or stiffness in the area. Or a person who completely loses track of present reality when confronted with stress can learn to repress only the emotions being experienced, but not cognitive awareness. At the same time that these symptomatic shifts are being created, it is important to continue the main therapeutic focus of working through to discover and reintegrate the dissociated material. Otherwise, the new suggestions only add another layer of obfuscation and continue the patient's lack of self-awareness. As the patient's self-awareness and integration increase, less and less hypnosis should occur. In general, the benefits of remaining fully conscious become self-rewarding. Any trauma survivor, however, no matter how well recovered, may temporarily lapse back into the dissociative defense at times of severe or unexpected stress.

Several hypnotic treatment techniques will be described below. As a means of organization, they are listed according to Judith Herman's (1991) sequence of treatment goals for working with trauma survivors: establishing safety, working through of trauma, and empowerment of the survivor.

Much of patients' sense of safety arises from their perception of the surrounding environment. To the extent that they feel no sense of control, they are unlikely to be able to focus on therapeutic change. Often, they feel as out of control of their own feelings as they do of the outside world; they complain of chronic anxiety, fear, and/or panic attacks. While working to change external factors that place patients at risk (such as continuing to live with the abuse perpetrator), it is important for therapists to also help patients achieve a greater sense of inner control. One means to this goal is to help the survivor establish the image of a safe place within the mind to which he or she can retreat when overwhelmed by affect. With or without hypnosis, the patient should be encouraged to picture this place as vividly as possible, and to practice going there. Practice needs to occur first when the patient is relatively calm, so that this response is easier to achieve later at times of stress. The nature of this safe place may vary widely, according to each person's unique history and associations. One of my patients who had been a truck driver selected the cab of an eighteen-wheeler truck, with sun glinting off the clean, shiny hood and the hum of a well-tuned diesel engine.

Another useful technique to establish the sense of safety is to use hypnosis or guided imagery to reestablish a more accurate sense of time perspective. Many survivors feel as if their abuse had just happened, even if it occurred years earlier. It can be helpful to take the patient back to the time of the abuse and then work slowly forward through time, noticing important events that have occurred along the way, either in the patient's own life or in the world at large. A person might note, for example, that since the trauma occurred he got his driver's license, finished high school, got a job, moved to another state, and so forth. In addition, a visual image may be helpful, with the trauma seen in the distant past as a very small image far away and with larger images of more recent events closer in the foreground.

Using a similar technique, survivors can be helped to stay more aware of current strengths, skills, and resources in their environment instead of being completely flooded by a regressed perception of helplessness. Reexperiencing successful events, picturing a large poster with a display of symbols of their strengths, imaging a valued authority figure reassuring them of their skills, and other such methods can all help the patient to a greater perception of safety.

Many survivors have a great fear of their own inner rage at their abuse. Even persons not suffering from multiple personality disorder may describe the sense of a monster inside struggling to get loose and wreak havoc. By approaching this "monster" with either hypnosis or guided imagery, it is possible to help the patient reframe this aspect of themselves as a protective ally who is there to serve the patient rather than to cause harm. Often, approaching this state of rage within the patient is harrowing for the therapist as well as the patient. Because the patient will pick up the therapist's attitude and beliefs about this situation, it is important that the therapist approach this work feeling confident that safety and control can be maintained. This confidence can occur secondary to the therapist's thorough knowledge of the patient's dynamics and likelihood of acting out. It is also possible to negotiate with the patient before doing this work as to arrangements by which both the patient and therapist can feel secure. This can involve having another person available to help maintain physical control, a hypnotic suggestion that the patient will not be able to leave the chair during this work, or even hospitalization to provide a safe working environment. Whatever the arrangement, it is important that the patient be an active collaborator with the therapist in its design. This fosters the suggestions that it is the patient's responsibility to remain safe and that the patient has the self-control to carry out this responsibility.

Hypnosis is particularly effective in helping patients alter self-destructive patterns and enhance their self-soothing capacity. Because of the vividness of the hypnotic experience, patients feeling the need to cut themselves or to act out in other ways can be taught to divert these urges to inner fantasy rather than real life. For example, one patient was discouraged at repeatedly breaking objects in her apartment in states of rage. She found a hypnotic image of breaking up huge rock piles with a sledgehammer, accompanied by pounding a real pillow, to be much more effective. In a similar fashion, self-soothing can be more vivid using hypnosis. Furthermore, working with the patient to develop self-soothing images can allow the therapist to model for the patient an attitude that such soothing is appropriate and normal. This can be important for survivors with little real-life experience in being soothed. Such images can be as simple as picturing oneself wrapped safely in a warm blanket, or as complex as swimming in magic ponds of sparkling water that clean away the effects of sexual abuse both inside and outside the body.

Finally, hypnosis can be used to enhance safety in crisis situations. With the patient's consent, a code word can be placed as a posthypnotic suggestion that will return the patient to a hypnotic trance when used. The therapist can use this code in person or over the phone when the patient is too dissociated or upset to focus on coping with the crisis. Once he or she is hypnotized, it is much easier to help the patient become calm and to discuss what further assistance is needed. If the patient suffers from multiple personality disorder or fugue states, a posthypnotic suggestion can be placed that part of the person will remain aware and take over consciousness if any potentially dangerous behavior is about to occur. As with other hypnotic work, it is important that the patient be an active participant in formulating these suggestions. Otherwise, these suggestions will represent an external force imposing control over the patient's feelings and behavior. This is easily perceived as a recapitulation of any abuse that the victim has endured. The patient may cooperate with the suggestions, but the sense of being a helpless victim is reinforced.

Working through the traumatic material is a major component of treatment of trauma survivors. As noted before, hypnosis allows access to dissociated states of consciousness in which primitive perceptions of the trauma are encapsulated. The first task is often to assist the patient to recover a general, intellectual sense of what trauma has occurred, placing it in the correct context of time and circumstances. Since trauma memories represent state-dependent learning (Tinnin, 1990), hypnosis can help the patient reenter the affective state in which the trauma occurred and then work back in time through other episodes in which the same affect occurred until the original traumatic material is reached.

John Watkins (1978) has developed the *affective-bridge technique* to accomplish this. For example, using this technique, a therapist might start with a feeling that the patient describes as nauseous anxiety each time she sees red food. The therapist would ask her to go back in time to each incident when she can recall this feeling occurring. By working back through time, the original traumatic event causing this reaction is eventually accessed. Sometimes the patient has a sense of the age at which the trauma occurred, but not the details; a standard hypnotic age regression to the target age can be helpful in this situation. At other times, the survivor may only remember certain details of the scene in which the trauma occurred. By returning the survivor under hypnosis to the scene, the patient can be encouraged to broaden the field of awareness gradually to include other details from the scene, and eventually the actions and feelings from this scene as well. Finally, in persons with strongly delineated ego states or multiple personality disorder, hypnosis can be used to gain access to the ego state that was present at the time of the trauma. This ego state can have full awareness of the trauma, while the normally conscious person is completely amnesic for the event.

Once the general memory of the event is retrieved, considerable further work is needed. The memory may exist in the form of jumbled fragments that need to be assembled to form a whole gestalt of the trauma, or reliving of the trauma in abreaction may be needed to integrate fully all the affective and cognitive content of the trauma. Finally, the material must be worked through to the point that the survivor has reintegrated this material totally into his or her normal level of consciousness with a realistic sense of perspective. In each of these tasks, hypnosis is helpful in that it allows realistic reliving of experience while maintaining at least a small portion of the self as an observing ego at the normal level of consciousness. In this way, material previously cut off in the alternative dissociated portions of consciousness becomes part of the normal consciousness as well, and integration is possible.

During the working-through process, spontaneous abreactions and/or intrusive flashbacks may occur as material from unconscious levels of awareness is stirred up. Hypnosis can provide a means of structure and control in these circumstances. If recall is occurring too quickly, suggestions of slowing down can be effective. Such suggestions can be as straightforward as saying, "The mind can go slower now. The more material there is, the slower the mind can go, as it is weighted down with all those memories." Other, more concrete suggestions can be useful, such as suggesting that each memory fragment is stored on videotape as it comes up, and that no matter how fast the memories get stored on the tape, the patient will see them played at normal speed and can even put the tape on hold if desired. In a similar fashion, affective distance can be produced if the patient is overwhelmed by the trauma. Suggestions might be made, for example, that the memory is viewed on a small television screen, and that the sound can be turned off if necessary. Finally, material can be repressed deliberately, if needed. This can occur if a session has to be ended before an abreaction is complete, or if a spontaneous abreaction begins in a situation where productive working through is not possible. Suggestions such as putting the memory in a locked safe, sinking it far down out of sight into the unconscious, and so forth are useful. The person should always be assured, however, that these memories will be returned to soon, when they can be dealt with effectively. This promise needs to be honored, or considerable unconscious resistance is likely. This can result in impulsive acting out (stemming from the unconscious) in an effort to be sure that the patient's long-ignored trauma is acknowledged.

Herman's (1991) empowerment phase of treatment involves helping patients become aware of their capacity to engage actively and successfully in life, and of a healthy sense of entitlement that they have the right to do so. This process actually begins early in treatment, as the patient experiences the capacity to be safe and learns to bring dissociation under conscious self-control. Hypnosis can be used to help the patient experience a preview of the future, sampling what it will feel like as current goals are actually accomplished. In addition, positive self-affirmation statements can be enhanced with hypnosis so that they command the same focus of attention as old messages of self-blame and shame instilled by the experience of trauma. A typical self-affirmation statement might be, "I'm going to take the best care I can of myself today, and I have the right to be safe." Finally, as noted in the section on safety, hypnosis can help the person to be more consistently aware of adult strengths and resources that might otherwise be overlooked due to the patient's habitual self-perception of weakness and helplessness.

Conclusion

Effective treatment of trauma requires that the therapist understand dissociative phenomena and the hypnotic mechanisms through which they occur. Using either formal hypnosis or informal suggestion, effective psychotherapy can enable trauma survivors to gain control over dissociation and regain an integrated perception of themselves in their world as self-empowered individuals rather than victims.

References

Bernstein, E. M., and F. W. Putnam (1986). Development, reliability, and validity of a dissociation scale. *Journal of Nervous and Mental Disease* 174 (no. 12):727–35.

Bliss, E. L. (1986). *Multiple Personality, Allied Disorders, and Hypnosis.* New York: Oxford University Press.

Fish-Murray, C. C., E. V. Koby, and B. van der Kolk. 1987. Evolving ideas: the effect of abuse on children's thought. In Bessel A. van der Kolk (Ed.), *Psychological Trauma,* Washington, DC: American Psychiatric Press. pp. 89–110.

Gruenewald, D. (1984). On the nature of multiple personality: comparisons with hypnosis. *International Journal of Clinical and Experimental Hypnosis* 32 (no. 2):170–90.

Herman, J. (1991). *Learning from Women.* Harvard Medical School Department of Continuing Education Course, Boston.

MacLean, P. (1973). *A Triune Concept of the Brain and Behavior.* Toronto: University of Toronto Press.

Spiegel, D. (1990). Trauma, dissociation, and hypnosis. In Richard P. Kluft (Ed.), *Incest-Related Syndromes of Adult Psychopathology,* Washington, DC: American Psychiatric Press, pp. 247–261.

Terr, L. C. (1991). Childhood traumas: an outline and overview. *American Journal of Psychiatry* 148 (no. 1):10–20.

Tinnin, L. (1990). Mental unity, altered states of consciousness and disso-
ciation. *Dissociation 3* (no. 3):154–59.
Watkins, J. G. (1978). *The Therapeutic Self: Developing Resonance—Key
to Effective Relationships.* New York: Human Sciences Press.
Watkins, J. G., and H. H. Watkins (1979). Ego states and hidden observers.
Journal of Altered States of Consciousness 5:3–18.

5

Psychopharmacology of the Abused

George M. Dominiak

We know little about the appropriate pharmacologic treatment of human reactions to abuse experiences. There is essentially no literature on the subject; the nearest research encompasses the study of post-traumatic stress disorder (PTSD). The patients of PTSD research are typically victims or perpetrators of war trauma, refugees of war, survivors of the Holocaust during World War II, or persons who had witnessed or suffered a singular tragic event. Pharmacologically speaking, what is notable about this body of work is the dramatically inconsistent response of various symptom clusters to medications. Given that this research is the closest approximation we have to the study of the effects of sexual traumatization, there is much for us to learn from these reports. Borrowing from the study of PTSD, other related work, and from clinical experience, the present chapter will attempt to suggest and elucidate pharmacologic approaches to the clinical manifestations of abuse reactions. The discussions will focus on assessment and treatment of symptoms rather than on categories of medications.

PTSD: A Heterogenous Grouping

In reviewing the literature on medication response in PTSD, (see Friedman 1988, and Davidson et al. 1990 for a good overview), one notices that in certain instances, people improve symptomatically. In other cases, the same medication shows no better response than placebo (Davidson, et al. 1990). Medication type does not seem to make much difference. Inconsistent and unpredictable responses appear to occur across a number of classes of medicines: tricyclic antidepressants, antidepressants of the monoamine oxidase inhibitor (MAOI) type, the anticonvulsant carbamazepine, the mood and aggression stabilizer lithium carbonate, neuroleptics, and benzodiazepines.

It is tempting to write off globally the variability in results as attributable to limitations or failings in research methodology. In fact, there are problems in this arena. Most of the work uses open clinical trials in which patients and clinicians are aware of the type of medication used; hence, a placebo comparison group is not included (see Lerer et al. 1987 as an example). Also, the use of appropriate control groups, a crossover paradigm blindly switching patients from one medication to another, and validated diagnostic and outcome measures varies greatly among the studies. It appears that limitations in research methodology alone make comparison or generalization from these reports very difficult. This does not mean, however, that the results reported in the work are not helpful when applied judiciously. In the clinical world, even knowing the extent of uncertainty in treatment response to medication is useful in helping us set our expectations.

Putting specific research design aside for a moment, there may be another complicating factor influencing unpredictability in outcome, this time a diagnostic one. PTSD is a powerful but puzzling phenomenon. Those who have had the opportunity to work with PTSD patients are aware of how complicated the treatments can be. Most noticeably this occurs because the patients, having suffered unmentionable horrors, are seemingly cursed to relive elements of the experiences time and time again. Different experiences or parts of events are recreated in therapy, with each recreation equally potent in its effects on the treatment process. The clinician's task is to bear the remembrances with the patients in the process of healing and reintegration. But there are so many variables in the treatment, so many levels of confusing clinical manifestations—for example, flashback experiences with hallucinations in the context of a distinct psychotic process.

Fortunately for us, patients with PTSD do have common features. These have been well described by many authors, but probably most clearly by Bessel van der Kolk and colleagues (van der Kolk 1984, 1987, 1988; van der Kolk et al. 1989). Describing clinical features, categorizing them, and labeling them helps us to maintain objectivity in the face of powerful clinical demands. The set of common features of patients with pathological trauma reactions has also been designated in the American Psychiatric Association's *Diagnostic and Statistical Manual of Mental Disorders* (DSM) as PTSD. These features include, of course, the experience of trauma, as well as features of intrusive "reexperiencing," symptoms characterized as avoidance of stimuli, and symptoms of increased arousal. Individuals who were found to have these DSM features were included in the medication research we are discussing.

It would be easy to assume, since we have diagnostic criteria that define actual common symptom clusters in individuals with PTSD, that patients with criteria-defined PTSD constitute a homogenous group. In fact, this assumption might not be true, which may account for inconsistency in outcomes. Regarding the PTSD research, with all the methodologic limitations put aside for the moment, the point here is that diagnostic heterogeneity may be the most significant confounding variable.

Whether or not a group of people categorically show symptoms that are diagnosable as PTSD, it seems likely that those who suffer war trauma, singular episodes of traumatic experience, or recurrent and persistent sexual victimization may show differences in presentation and response to medication or other treatments. The syndrome of PTSD can be arrived at via countless traumatic pathways. As if things are not complicated enough, etiologic heterogeneity, though undoubtedly very important, is itself just one among many variables accounting for unpredictable outcome.

PTSD and Outcome: Variables to Keep in Mind

The word *outcome* is used here not just as a reference to medication response but also more generally as including variations in symptom presentation or symptom outcome (that is, different symptomatic response to the same trauma). For example, DSM-defined PTSD is one possible outcome of traumatic experience. Some factors that might influence variability in outcome, in the general sense used here, include type of trauma, relationship with the perpetrator, amount of time that has passed since the trauma, duration of symptom manifestations, quality of available social supports near the time of the trauma, and comorbidity of personality disorder. All these can influence the clinical picture that may develop, as well as the response to treatment.

Also, regarding medication trials, the presence of other DSM Axis I psychopathology or a predisposition may account for a positive response in some patients. In other words, PTSD patients with predisposition to or actual major depression may respond in a general fashion to tricyclic or MAOI compounds. Other PTSD patients with behavioral dyscontrol may respond to lithium carbonate or carbamazepine; those with cognitive disorganization may respond to neuroleptics. Regarding the variable of personality disorder, it is an unfortunate truth that we have essentially no research-based predictive knowledge of the interaction of personality characteristics with other psychopathology categories as they affect PTSD. On the other hand, our clinical experience tells us that the interaction of personality variables and treatment is powerful (Tobin and Johnson 1991).

Regarding diagnosis, the customary use of DSM criteria for PTSD creates an air of commonality when applied to this group of patients. It is important to remember that the DSM is more descriptive categorization and observation labeling than it is "truth" about psychological process. With differences in the nature of traumatic etiology, concurrent psychopathology, and/or predisposition, it is not surprising that research groups of patients respond unpredictably to various medications.

Indications for Psychopharmacology Referral

Regardless of our clinical discipline, every clinician of severely disturbed abuse victims has the responsibility of ongoing clinical assessment. Typically, evaluation and reevaluation are woven into the fabric of our psychotherapeutic work. What to respond to, what to explore further, what to postpone, what to integrate, what to examine in our own reactions—these are but a few of the questions we ask ourselves constantly during therapy. At some point in time, the issue of referral for psychopharmacological evaluation will arise. This is not a simple matter for either the therapist or the consulting psychiatrist, because of its significance to the treatment and possible meaning to the patient.

When medication evaluation becomes a consideration, an entirely new set of questions is opened. The danger is that the mind-set of the therapist may shift from the flow of the therapy or evaluation process. This development is all too common among practitioners today. Frequently, as a supervisor one hears from a therapist, "She wasn't doing so well controlling her crying, so I mentioned that I was worried about her. I told her maybe she should see Dr. X for meds, and that I would schedule an appointment for her." The subject of medications is presented here as a necessity, a reaction to a symptom, with little exploration. Others say, "She has severe PTSD and she dissociates a lot, so I'm referring her for medication assessment." Let us now take a closer look at the process of deciding upon referral, at some of its underlying assumptions and potential effects on the clinical work.

A common belief among clinicians today is that the discovery of a history of severe sexual abuse in the context of other psychopathology indicates a high probability that medication will be needed. Often, the evaluation process and the necessary efforts of developing a working alliance are suddenly given second priority to getting the patient evaluated pharmacologically. This concern is, of course, not applicable to cases of potentially life-threatening crises, when active intervention is required. When the immediate safety of the patient or others is not jeopardized, however, other factors should be given consideration prior to referral. These include the patient's fears and prejudices about use of chemical agents, pressures from family and significant others, the opinions of other treaters, and financial and other practical concerns, such as transportation or a need for monitoring of medication use. A hastened disruptive referral, however well-meaning it may be, is doomed to failure without adequate attention given to management considerations and psychodynamic impact. This would be especially true for new patients who have not had time enough to develop trust in their therapist, clinic, or treatment system. The comments that follow regarding pharmacologic referral assume these variables have been addressed prior to consultation.

When should the patient be referred for medication evaluation? Most typically, this occurs during the initial workup or ongoing treatment when the therapist "feels" the limitations of psychosocial (including behavioral and hypnotic) interventions. Other occasions include periods when clinicians find themselves unable to influence, modulate, or tolerate (a legitimate consideration) the patient's symptoms and suffering. There are also other circumstances, such as when the patient's affective, cognitive, or behavioral dyscontrol continue to grow and the words of the therapist and the therapeutic relationship no longer appear capable of safely "holding" the patient. A final few considerations might include the patient's or family's wish to have an evaluation, or the case of sudden, unpredictable, or emergent changes in symptoms that persist.

One should keep in mind that clinical research has shown no good evidence of remission of chronic traumatic reactions through the use of medications alone. This statement requires some qualification, in that it is common to see the symptoms of a stress reaction improved by the successful treatment of an underlying major depression or brief reactive psychosis. In the absence of another major psychopathological process that typically responds to pharmacologic agents, however, the use of psychotropic medication most commonly serves as an adjunct or facilitator of psychosocial interventions via symptom relief. Often, patients freed from anxiety or fatigue from insomnia may find themselves thinking more clearly, psychologically reinforced, and better able to integrate their thoughts and experiences in the therapy. In the face of extreme and relentless disturbance in anxiety, affect, behavior and cognition, however, the need for pharmacologic evaluation is rarely subtle. But in almost every case, this turn in the treatment requires some preparatory work. It may take the form of verbal exploration, information sharing, or at times practical help in following through with the appointment.

Clinical experience teaches us that in almost no case of a severely abused individual is pharmacologic treatment simple, devoid of potential harm, or removed from psychological effects. The introduction of another person (the psychopharmacologist) and medications into the treatment is a significant intervention, with consequences to be borne in the psychotherapy. Bringing drug treatment into the work makes a powerful statement about hope, the severity of the psychopathology, and the limitations of the therapeutic relationship.

Gunderson (1984) describes a number of possible transference complications of initiating pharmacotherapy in the treatment of patients with borderline personality disorder; his insights could be applied fairly to the treatments of any patients with difficulties forming trusting relationships or with problems of regulating self-esteem. One complication mentioned by Gunderson is that the patient may develop the idea that he or she has failed in therapy by not having responded adequately to the therapist's efforts. Another danger is the perception, real or imagined, on the part of the patient that the treatment relationship has become intolerable to the therapist. In this case, the therapist is seen by the patient as wanting to distance from, withdraw from, or metaphorically "abandon" the work. The patient may believe the therapist thinks of him or her as hopelessly defective or somehow repugnant. On many occasions during consultation, I have heard from a tearful patient feelings that he or she must be horribly damaged and will never get better, and that this is why he or she was sent by the therapist. In these patients' minds, the suggestion of referral became essentially the equivalent of feeling the therapist give up on them.

When the therapist's intentions about psychopharmacology consultation and the patient's hopes and fears are not adequately integrated into the therapeutic process, complications may arise. For example, feelings of abandonment and of oneself as hopelessly damaged, if unaddressed, may lead to resistance in the evaluation, refusal to take medication even if clearly indicated, or poor compliance with a pharmacologic regimen. Disregarding the patient's hidden concerns may be costly in terms of outcome.

Addressing these issues lies in the domain of the psychotherapy and should not be left for the pharmacologist to deal with. Certainly, any experienced consultant will be sensitive to fears and psychodynamic consequences; however, as a new person in the patient's clinical management, he or she is disadvantaged by the frailty of the developing working alliance. Since many of the patient's fears or misattributions about the meaning of the referral derive in part from feelings about the therapist or what are perceived to be the therapist's motives, the issues must be dealt with directly and openly in the psychotherapeutic relationship. In some cases the consultant would do well by postponing pharmacotherapy, referring the patient back to the therapist, and waiting until the scenario is more favorable for introducing medications. If nothing else, this reinforces the priority of the psychotherapeutic work.

Aside from clinical emergencies, timing in introducing medications seems very important. As mentioned, delaying the intervention is often therapeutically useful. The task of pacing becomes even more difficult in cases when the patient personally requests evaluation for symptom relief. Experience teaches that the patient is best served when the request is considered at two levels: first, at face value, and second, as a product or symptom of the treatment. The challenge to the therapist is to be loyal to therapeutic process, yet responsive to the conscious needs of the patient.

Patients have described numerous motives beyond simple symptom reduction for requesting medication. These include pleasing their family, pleasing the therapist, giving up on their own attempts at symptom regulation, expressing dissatisfaction at their clinical progress, or showing disappointment in the therapist.

Gina, a twenty-seven-year-old single professional woman with a history of both physical and sexual abuse in adolescence, unpredictably demanded that I give her medication to control her anxiety. She had never asked for medication in eighteen months of working together in twice-weekly therapy. In fact, she appeared to be doing particularly well during the weeks prior to this new demand. I told her I was very interested in her request and wanted to first explore things a bit. She reacted with hurt and anger, accusing me of being insensitive to her needs and not realizing how difficult it was for her to speak up for herself at all.

At first, I was taken aback. Feeling guilty, I wondered to myself if perhaps I was being cold and unresponsive. After talking about her symptoms, however, I decided not to change course and suggested that we spend some time trying to learn what had changed that was causing her to feel more anxiety. For a number of sessions, she continued to express hurt and disappointment in my being just like "the other men" in her life who left her to suffer alone. I then somehow realized that two weeks prior to her demand, we had changed our previously fixed session times at my request. Upon inquiry, she recalled that this was when she began feeling more anxiety. As it turned out, she was enormously hurt by my request to change our meeting time, which she felt she could not refuse. She described feeling that I thought she was doing better than she was. The request for new times was, in her mind, a first step in an imagined plan to replace her with a new, more interesting patient. As she saw it, giving her medications would be an admission on my part that she was as ill as ever and deserved this special attention.

In the case of Gina, responding to the immediate demand for help from medication would have supported an avoidance of an important interpersonal development. It would have served as a distraction from active but unaddressed therapeutic issues. Delay and exploration proved fruitful, even though medication would have probably calmed her anxiety.

In general, it seems fair to assume that patients with a history of significant abuse are extremely sensitive to change and to any experience that could be interpreted as the application of external control. This appears to be true even when their own behavior or demands generate the change. The misperception of the thoughtful decision to recommend psychopharmacologic evaluation as intrusive or controlling, even when initiated by the patient, is an ever-present possibility. Our patients' sensitivities regarding these matters, except of course in times of extreme risk of personal harm, should be understood and addressed. Suggesting the use of psychotropic medications is a clear and powerful clinical statement. The point to be emphasized is that the process of referral itself can heal or hurt independent, of the ultimate neuropharmacologic outcome.

Symptoms and Psychopharmacology

Symptoms, symptom clusters, syndromes, and their etiologies and interactions are the targets of pharmacologic evaluation. They are rarely found in pure form. Further complicating matters is the nature of human adaptation to recurrent trauma. For example, a longstanding adjustment to trauma such as chronic depression may become overshadowed by current reactions to memories such as agitation or promiscuity. Mistrust obstructs the patient-physician alliance. Dissociation shields symptoms from the clinician's view. The work of the pharmacologist is limited by what can be seen, heard, and felt and by intuitive capacity. Needless to say, when the patient has the proclivity to deny, dissociate, minimize, and forget (all to her or his distinct psychological advantage), the psychiatrist's task becomes formidable.

For traumatized individuals, many of the usual assumptions about symptoms do not apply. For example, the presence of hallucinations may not indicate psychosis, depression may not be major affective disorder, episodic overwhelming anxiety may not be panic, and hypomanic agitation may not be bipolar disorder. Each traumatized patient should be considered a case of one—distinct, specific, and psychologically organized into a unique system. New diagnostic and pharmacologic rules often need to be developed that are specific to the individual.

The remainder of this chapter will review specific categories of symptoms as seen in victims of abuse. Pharmacologic suggestions and caveats will be presented only to serve as guides through the confusion most of us feel in evaluating and treating these patients.

Anxiety and Panic

Perhaps the most ubiquitous of symptoms found in individuals with trauma histories is anxiety. It can manifest in a variety of ways, for example, as generalized jitteriness or tremulousness; simple uneasiness; irritability; intolerance of overstimulation from noise, strong odors, or other sources; or as various forms of panic episodes. The amount of discomfort experienced by patients may also vary widely. If of long duration, anxiety may lead to lowered appetite, social avoidance, apathy, somatic complaints, and the development of a depressive syndrome. A commonly seen sequence begins with anxiety symptoms that exacerbate and lead to a full anxiety syndrome/disorder that then may go on to depressive symptoms and major depression. At some point in this anxiety-to-depression continuum, it becomes impossible to distinguish cause and effect. Depressive symptoms that might previously have been remedied by treating the anxiety are no longer responsive; the depression becomes primary. Presently, we have no predictable way of distinguishing the two adequately. It is encouraging, however, that successful treatment of depression will typically relieve anxiety symptoms.

There is another controversy here. The question that remains to be answered is whether the anxiety of depression in a nontraumatized individual is identical phenomenologically or neurobiologically to the anxiety of the stress disorder of the sexually abused? It is also unclear whether the anxiety symptoms of the severely sexually abused differ from the anxiety of post-traumatic stress disorder of other trauma, such as combat experiences. Friedman (1988) writes: "To summarize, PTSD, major depression, and panic disorder all appear to have unique biological profiles despite considerable overlap in symptoms and responsivity to tricyclics and MAOIs" (p. 284). Though addressing these issues is beyond the scope of this chapter, it is important for the reader of the sections that follow to be aware of the influence of potential heterogeneity on treatment decisions and response.

Anxiety symptoms and their common correlate, insomnia, generally signal a disruption in the patient's ability to adapt to increasing psychological demands. This is a psychodynamic representation of the etiology of anxiety. Biopsychiatrists may object, saying that anxiety disorders are biologically generated, in particular in the case of post-traumatic stress disorder with its concomitant hyperarousal of the autonomic nervous system. From either perspective, an imaginary threshold of stimulus or stress tolerance exists that is more readily surpassed than in the "normal" or usual condition.

In the case of sexual traumatization, certain special circumstances exist. Individuals may develop unsettling intrusive internal experiences, vivid recollections of traumatic moments, and a resulting sense of loss of control of their thought processes. This is seen when a patient is just coming to awareness of previously suppressed or repressed traumatic memories or during periods of regression in therapy, generalized dyscontrol, or the development of major depression with secondary anxiety symptoms (the opposite of the anxiety-to-depression continuum described above). Any destabilization of emotional controls, such as depression or retraumatization, may overwhelm the patient's usual capability to adapt psychologically, leading to anxiety or panic symptoms.

The usual methods of treating anxiety include psychological interventions aimed at reinforcing adaptive skills, teaching specific relaxation techniques, and utilizing distraction and social contact as a means of soothing and comfort, as well as pharmacologic approaches. Regarding medication, three classes of drugs have been used widely for anxiety management: benzodiazepines, antidepressants, and neuroleptics. The benzodiazepines are exceedingly effective in quieting anxiety symptoms almost immediately. They are well tolerated by most patients and, except for sedation, in small doses cause few early side effects.

Unfortunately for patients with severe anxiety requiring substantial doses, some will experience troublesome reactions that may potentially inhibit the psychotherapeutic process by affecting memory, disinhibiting behavior, and eliminating useful internal affective cues via numbing of feelings. Specifically, physiologic tolerance, psychological and physiologic dependence, medication-induced amnesia, behavioral disinhibition, and postsedation hyperarousal and irritability from dropping serum levels, common with relatively shorter-acting compounds such as alprazolam (Xanax) and lorazepam (Ativan), are among the most problematic side effects. Judicious use of modest amounts of benzodiazepines, however, can be invaluable in calming certain patients enough to allow them much needed nighttime rest and the overall experience of feeling more capable of tolerating stressful internal and environmental demands.

Antidepressant medications are also effective in treating more severe anxiety states, especially if the latter are complicated by depressive symptomatology. Like the benzodiazepines, antidepressants generally improve insomnia. Problems arise in that patients may have to wait weeks for a complete medication response, side effects are common with all antidepressant types, and essentially all antidepressants with the exception of trazodone (Desyrel) and fluoxetine (Prozac) carry significant potential for lethal consequences from overdose.

Paradoxical reactions, as with the benzodiazepines, are often seen. Most common is a lack of sedative effect, with resulting agitation, increased anxiety symptoms, and rarely (with the tricyclics and fluoxetine or Prozac) a neurolepticlike effect of akathisia or motor restlessness. This agitation most often occurs at the beginning of treatment. It is most common with what are referred to as the "energizing antidepressants"—bupropion (Wellbutrin), fluoxetine (Prozac), desipramine (Norpramin), and to some degree nortriptyline (Pamelor)—but can occur with all antidepressants, including monoamine oxidase inhibitors such as tranylcypromine (Parnate) and phenelzine (Nardil).

To avoid the possibility of agitation, the psychiatrist might try starting the antidepressant initially with very small doses that are increased more gradually than usual. The patients should, of course, be forewarned of this possible reaction. If the agitation and reactive anxiety are intolerable to the patient and antidepressant treatment is clearly indicated, a benzodiazepine (preferably a longer-acting type to minimize frequency of dosing) may be added. It is rare to find an individual who shows paradoxical agitation to both antidepressants and benzodiazepines.

Some patients suffer anxiety to such an extent that cognitive processes are affected. Racing thoughts, confusion, intense rumination, and preoccupation with or without depression may accompany the anxiety or episodically arise as a concurrent reaction. Some patients, especially those with significant personality disorder in addition to trauma reactions and anxiety, may periodically need more than amelioration of anxiety with benzodiazepines and may find themselves feeling more hostile and irritable when treated with tricyclic antidepressants. Paranoia and other psychotic features may accompany the anxiety episodes.

Carefully planned use of a time-limited regimen of low-dose neuroleptics has been found to be helpful in a select group of abused patients. For example, perphenazine (Trilafon) in doses of 2 to 12 mg daily or thioridazine (Mellaril) in doses of 25 to 150 mg daily for a four- to eight-week trial period is the cautious recommendation. Extreme care with these drugs is warranted, because of potentially life-threatening or permanent side effects in addition to their ability to numb affect and inhibit the patient's thought production. When effective, the relief felt by patients is dramatic and occurs within a few days. They often describe feeling serene, more in control of their thoughts and emotions (particularly anger), and more optimistic about being able to overcome their tremendous intensity of affect and internal confusion.

Panic anxiety is a common symptom experienced by victims of sexual abuse. For some individuals, panic episodes appear to be autonomous (that is, unrelated to specific experiences) and are indistinguishable clinically from formal DSM panic disorder in non-traumatized patients. In others it may be triggered by specific memories, misidentifications of people and places seen as similar to those associated with the patient's abuse, or specific kinds of demands in social settings or the workplace. In both primary and secondary panic, the treatment is similar and is determined by the frequency of attacks and the amount of disruption in functioning that results.

Over time, if left untreated, patients develop extreme fear of recurrent panic attacks, at times vigilantly avoiding what they perceive to be triggers. On clinical grounds these patients may appear to have agoraphobic tendencies, but again this seems to be a self-protective secondary fear rather than a primary phobia of open places and social gatherings. Patients have described not having suffered panic attacks for months, yet feeling crippled by the anticipatory anxiety of a recurrence of panic. Many patients can experience dramatic relief of both anxiety associated with panic and panic itself by taking a high-potency, long-acting benzodiazepine in small doses—for example, clonazepam (Klonopin) in doses of 0.5 mg once or twice daily. Others will require a higher-dose regimen of benzodiazepines or a trial of antidepressants to obtain relief.

Other atypical forms of anxiety in trauma victims include the panic associated with eating in anorexic patients and with the urge to binge and purge in bulimic individuals. The anxiety felt here is often quite powerful and typically dictates the person's behavior. No medication has been found to be effective in treating anorexia nervosa, though small occasional doses of short-acting benzodiazepines, such as alprazolam (Xanax) and lorazepam (Ativan), have been helpful in rare instances during periods of attempted refeeding in a hospital setting. Regarding bulimic patients, benzodiazepines are generally avoided, because many of these individuals have tendencies toward chemical dependency. Individual and group treatments geared specifically to addressing the issues of bulimia have been found effective. Pharmacologically, it appears that antidepressant medication of any type can be helpful as an adjunct to psychotherapy, even in bulimics with no depressive symptoms. Given that bulimia tends to be a recurring and episodic disorder, however, the long-term benefits of medication remain somewhat suspect.

In evaluating anxiety and panic in sexually traumatized patients, one should carefully assess the presence or absence of substance abuse. This would include nicotine, caffeine, alcohol, and so-called recreational street drugs as well as "hard" drugs. Alcohol, cocaine, marijuana, and caffeine are of particular concern in that they can generate and exacerbate anxiety or panic symptoms. The nonsense of pharmacotherapy while symptoms are potentially being stimulated exogenously is obvious.

Also, substituting prescribed drugs for nonprescription dependencies (for example, benzodiazepines for alcohol) rarely succeeds in the long term without treating the substance abuse directly and adding Alcoholics Anonymous or other organized treatment/support structures to the patient's treatment plan. Only if the patient uses alcohol or chemicals purely for self-medication of anxiety or depressive symptoms will substance abuse stop after detoxification and appropriate treatment. This, however, is an unusual occurrence. Assessment of substance abuse should be ongoing, even after an apparently trusting treatment relationship has been developed.

The Depressions

The term *depression*, as it is used commonly by clinicians of the sexually abused, refers to a spectrum of clinical presentations. Unfortunately, too often it is employed as a synonym for dysphoria of any type. This situation is complicated by the fact that a certain amount of mood dysregulation is expected. Also, manifestations of depression in traumatized patients more often than not fall into the DSM category of atypical. Abreactive experiences, agitation, anxiety states, despair, and negativity of thought are common in the abused and may not represent depression as the psychiatrist might usually see it. In this section of the chapter, an attempt will be made to describe, through oversimplification, categories of depression specific to sexually abused individuals, with an emphasis on pharmacologic assessment.

The kind of symptom picture most typically responsive to antidepressant medication is one of overall mood and affect dysregulation. Basic biological and social functions such as appetite, sleep, capacity for pleasure, levels of motivation and interest, activity, and concentration are disrupted. The patient experiences an internal change, often making comments such as, "This isn't me." Patients will have made attempts to pull themselves out from their unhappiness by overemphasizing activities, spending, vacations, and in those with impulsive tendencies, through the use of alcohol, drugs, sex, overeating, and other forms of dyscontrol. If one believes that a possible etiology (among others) for depression is that of a final outcome from failed attempts at adaptation to persistent stressors and recurrent or multiple experiences of loss, than it becomes clear how traumatized individuals pressured by continuous internal tension may be more susceptible than others.

Treatment of depression in the abused individual is particularly important in facilitating the psychotherapeutic process. Mood dysregulation, whether depression or mania, leads to increased dyscontrol of anxiety management and may directly alter the capacity for behavioral control. In impulsive and self-destructive individuals, the disruption of mood disorder often adversely affects the person's sense of self-control and concomitant self-esteem. If one takes the therapist's perspective, a certain amount of sadness can aid the process of self-reflection in therapy (Gut 1989); also, some loosening of emotional controls can lead to acceptance of uncomfortable affects such as anger or hate at perpetrators or those that failed to protect. Major depression, however, when present for an extended period of time is more disabling, distracting, and potentially dangerous than helpful.

The first type of depression seen in the abused individual is not the most common but is in some ways prototypical of major depression as we know it. This is depression of the melancholic type. The patient presents as being emotionally, physically, motivationally, and to some extent cognitively "shut down." The patient thinks, moves, and speaks slowly. When melancholia has psychotic elements, it may be confused with catatonic states. This is the classic neurovegetative depression. Medications and hospitalization are often necessary, as the patient becomes nonfunctional, apathetic, and irritable. Clinical response is typically excellent. Almost any tricyclic antidepressant or MAOI is helpful if given in adequate doses and for appropriate durations. In assessing these patients and following them through recovery, one has a clear sense of a biological disturbance.

The second depressive type is what is seen most commonly in clinical practice with abused individuals. This is depression with agitation characterized most simply as a state of "misery." The patients are restless, anxious, sad, confused, unable to relax, and preoccupied with unhappy thoughts. They cannot easily concentrate but make valiant attempts at keeping themselves functional. Often the thought of taking medication early in the course of this type of depression is experienced by patients as a failure in personally managing their lives. Diagnostic confusion can arise here in that patients who are just beginning to address directly issues of their abuse and how it affects their lives may appear to have a similar symptom picture of hyperarousal, hypervigilance, and irritability without it being depression in a "true" sense. Time in therapy may be the most productive way to help the patient through this. It is when the patient feels exhausted from the anxiety and almost constant effort at self-regulation, or if by history the agitation leads to an increased risk of self-destructive behavior, that pharmacologic intervention might be attempted. During this agitated kind of depression, abused patients may be more susceptible to moments of extreme unhappiness, nightmares, and dissociation-related experiences.

Pharmacologic treatment is not simple for this kind of depressed state. A reasonable first attempt is the use of a sedating antidepressant such as trimipramine (Surmontil), imipramine (Tofranil), amitriptyline (Elavil), or if obsessionality is evident, clomipramine (Anafranil). The difficulty arises in that most patients have initial increased agitation or other uncomfortable side effects that may lead them to feel even more hopeless about feeling better. It is necessary to increase the doses fairly slowly to minimize annoying side effects and to explain how long one may have to wait before a significant medication response may occur.

The insomnia that accompanies depression with agitation is often severe and unresponsive to antidepressants alone until later in treatment. Often, benzodiazepines, relaxation exercises, or doses of trazodone (Desyrel) may be necessary. If racing thoughts and confusional states are present, a brief (four- to six-week) trial of low-dose neuroleptics is sometimes helpful until the depression improves. Often these patients suddenly find themselves taking three or more medications: an antidepressant, a tranquilizer, a neuroleptic, and perhaps an anticholinergic agent for side effects of the neuroleptic. This is a difficult, if not humiliating, experience for patients who may have functioned quite successfully prior to treatment and recognition of their abuse history. Much supportive counseling is necessary to maintain compliance and combat discouragement through difficult phases in the illness.

If the patient is not significantly improved after three months of such a treatment regimen, changing the antidepressant is indicated. If the patient refuses further trials of tricyclics, a monoamine oxidase inhibitor, or fluoxetine (Prozac) because of fears of side effects, bupropion (Wellbutrin) might be suggested, or embellishment of the tricyclic with lithium or thyroid hormone might be an alternate intervention. The reader may notice that trazodone (Desyrel) was not mentioned as a first-choice medication. Though trazodone is known to be only intermediate in antidepressant potency, it may be effective in some patients who cannot tolerate the side effects of other medications. It is outstanding in the treatment of insomnia. Its effectiveness in severe depressions of the type described here, however, has not been proven.

Though the literature does mention various ways of embellishing the effects of antidepressants (Roose and Glassman 1990), the most effective is through the use of lithium carbonate in doses that lead to fairly low serum levels of 0.4 to 0.8 mEq/L. The response may occur within days and can be at times dramatic. Also, with the kind of improvement seen, often neuroleptic medications can be stopped safely and tranquilizers slowly withdrawn. The literature is not very supportive of using thyroid hormone as an enhancer of antidepressant effect. If impulsivity is a problem and patients cannot tolerate lithium, carbamazepine (Tegretol) or divalproex sodium (Depakote) may be tried, with caution, in addition to the tricyclic.

A third type of depressive experience often seen in consultation is manifested as episodes of despair. These are described by patients as periods of deep unhappiness, hopelessness, and emptiness, plus anxiety to near-panic proportions that may last for minutes to hours. They are unlike panic attacks, with which these patients are often familiar. Without a context of general affective dysregulation, despair of this type should be treated psychosocially with ongoing therapy but with some addressing of the cognitive elements of the experience. In particular, the negative self-referential thinking in these moments (such as ideas of being evil or damaged) might be discussed. Relaxation techniques, distraction, and use of social contact are other suggestions. If the patient's unhappiness seems beyond shifts in psychological management, treating the anxiety episodically might be preferable to beginning an ongoing regimen of antidepressant trials. In extreme cases, where cognitive dysregulation occurs and elements of psychosis are apparent, the unfortunate need for small doses of neuroleptic medication arises and should be judiciously considered.

Chronic unhappiness is another common complaint of abuse victims. Here, the relative severity of the symptoms must be weighed against the emotional and physiologic cost of antidepressant trials. Dysthymia is not predictably responsive to medication, though exacerbations to major depression should be monitored.

Aside from the physical complications of side effects and the well-described psychological ramifications of using medications, there are clear dangers both in prescribing and not prescribing medications to depressed and potentially suicidal individuals. We give our patients toxic substances and must ensure their safety as best we can. Also, as is well-known to psychopharmacologists, the energy levels of our depressed patients may improve before their negative thinking and feelings of hopelessness. Under these circumstances, suicidal thoughts may persist in someone who has more energy to act but remains cognitively depressed. This can occur with any antidepressant. A given patient's potential for self destruction and overall impulsivity must be assessed continuously. Usually, a safeguard mechanism for interpersonal contact when impulses arise has been helpful. Often, friends or significant others are happy to be available if they know they have access to help from the psychiatrist or a form of emergency service if they feel overwhelmed or frightened.

Psychotic Phenomena

Clinical experience has taught us that there are countless pathways leading to the development of psychotic symptomatology. Not all psychosis is schizophrenia or delusional disorder. Toxic delirium, overdose, drug withdrawal, stroke, anorexia, grief, exhaustion, depression, mania, and drastic environmental deprivation or change are included (among others) in the list of etiological possibilities. Some of these, like bipolar disorder or schizophrenia, appear to be primary sources of psychosis. In other circumstances, psychotic symptoms develop as a reaction to biological or psychosocial influences; that is, the psychosis is secondary. Psychosis, like depression or anxiety, appears to be a potential common end point to extreme biological and social duress, a kind of capability intrinsic to human psychological functioning.

If one believes that psychotic symptoms represent a final pathway of response to psychological duress and vulnerability, it is remarkable how infrequently fulminant psychosis develops in cases of brutal sexual abuse. Instead, the mind appears to avoid a psychotic outcome through dissociation and other cognitive and psychological mechanisms. Unfortunately, psychotic-like symptoms do occur fairly frequently in severely disturbed abused patients. The difficult task for the psychopharmacologist is to attempt to distinguish true psychotic phenomena from symptoms that may appear to be psychosis but are attributable to dissociation, splitting, intrusive thoughts, vivid recollections, obsessionality, and extreme emotional reactions.

Diagnosing is not simple. For example, hallucination in the absence of toxicity or delirium was once considered a hallmark of schizophrenia. Asaad (1990), in reviewing the literature on hallucination, reminds us of research showing that only 66 percent of a group of schizophrenics were found to have hallucinations. He recommends that this symptom not be seen as diagnostically specific. Paranoia, fixed beliefs or delusional thinking, and confusional states are also nonspecific.

How, then, does the psychiatrist approach the diagnostic dilemma presented by an adult female patient with a history of longstanding sexual abuse in childhood and adolescence who complains of self-deprecating and potentially dangerous command hallucinations? First, fundamental details of history addressing the possible etiology of the hallucinations must be considered. How did they develop? Was their onset sudden or gradual? Have there been any changes in intensity? Did they develop in the context of substance abuse, depression, manic excitement, or biological illness? What of the patient's overall level of functioning over the past few years, including career competence, social life, and self-care skills? Are there familiar elements in the hallucinations that the patient relates to her abuse experiences? Is she prone to dissociative experiences? Does she manifest multiple or partial multiple personalities? These are but some of the questions that warrant attention. An important issue to address is the relationship of the psychotic symptom(s) to the patient's overall cognitive, psychological, and behavioral functioning.

If the patient shows signs of global deterioration without overriding elements of traumatic stress disorder and a psychotic process is evident, treatment should proceed as quickly as possible. First, all obvious underlying pathology, biological and psychological, must be addressed. This would include detoxification, overdose reactions, bipolar illness, and depression, to name but a few. Next, the patient should be comforted, kept safe, and treated vigorously with the appropriate antipsychotic medication.

If, however, the clinical picture does not include major affective disorder or generalized disruption in thought or daily functioning, other considerations require attention. The presence of hallucinations, paranoia, or fixed beliefs do not of themselves warrant a recommendation of treatment with antipsychotic medication. If these symptoms have arisen from a clinical picture of increasingly frequent intrusive memories, depersonalization, dissociative experiences, extreme apprehension, and anxiety, then psychosis would not be diagnosed. A first intervention would be to talk with the patient. Share your clinical concerns with the patient but in a manner that would reassure her that it does not appear she is losing her mind. If you think it might be helpful, explain to her that these kinds of experiences are not uncommon in individuals who have been abused.

In considering pharmacotherapy, keep in mind that dissociative states, intrusive recollections, flashbacks, and fragments of abuse events returning as auditory hallucinations are usually not very responsive to neuroleptic medication in the long term. In a crisis situation, however, antipsychotic drugs can be effective in sedating the patient, slowing racing thoughts and quieting inner experiences by numbing affect. The cost of their use is postponement of psychological growth and the possibility of dangerous toxic side effects. Other medications, such as benzodiazepines, are available to calm the patient with less overall risk. If the hallucinatory experience is associated with chronic severe personality disorder, however, and the psychotic symptomatology appears to be growing in its disruptive capacity or dangerous behavioral dyscontrol appears imminent, then small doses of a neuroleptic over a limited trial period may be necessary or even lifesaving.

In treating the sexually abused, all psychopharmacologic attempts are best made in the service of preserving the patient's sense of self-control. The goal is to reinforce the patient's internal controls, which supports her attempts at working through difficulties in psychotherapy or hypnotherapy.

Dissociative Phenomena and Intrusions

Though known for centuries, dissociation had been labeled and best described by Pierre Janet in 1889 (van der Kolk and van der Hart 1989). It was presented by Janet as a key psychological process in the human reaction to severe traumatic experience. For some reason, except as a component of hysterical reactions, dissociation was not given much emphasis in contemporary studies of psychopathology nor in developmental theories of personality disorder. Since the Vietnam War, however, clinicians and researchers have grown puzzled by reactions to combat trauma. During the same period, heightened awareness of the role of sexual abuse in the development of psychopathology (and multiple personality disorder in particular) has led to renewed interest in dissociation as a pathological process. But is it a pathological mechanism? Recent data seems to suggest that in a randomly selected group of adults, dissociative experiences are fairly common (Ross, Shaun, and Currie 1990).

The definition of dissociation used here is similar to that of Ludwig (1983): "Dissociation represents a process whereby certain mental functions which are ordinarily integrated with other functions presumably operate in a more compartmentalized or automatic way usually outside the sphere of conscious awareness or memory recall" (p. 93). In other words, the continuity of conscious experience is altered or disrupted. Elements of experience (including complete memories, bits of factual information, affects, or complete modes/states of relating) are shifted out of conscious awareness. In other cases, they are active in parallel with but split off from what is presently conscious. Dissociations may manifest as shifts in the general affective state, mood, or perspective of the individual. What is split off may then return to consciousness as an intrusion that then generates its own reactions in the individual. Confusion, anxiety, fear of psychic disorganization (quite different than psychotic fragmentation), and an experience of loss of internal control are common responses.

In the face of traumatic experience, normal methods of information processing become incapable of adapting to the enormity of the individual's reaction (van der Kolk and van der Hart 1989). In essence, the mind becomes overloaded and fragments (or dissociates) elements of the experience and its reactions. Finding similarities to the traumatic events in future experiences may reawaken the split-off memory and experience fragments. Because of the usually horrific nature of abuse experiences, these remembrances are felt as unwanted, horrible intrusions. The patient may again call into play dissociative mechanisms as the remembered events attempt to rise to conscious awareness.

Because of the extent of suffering, at first glance it may be difficult to see dissociative mechanisms as normal attempts at adaptation. Offhandedly, many clinicians still believe dissociation is pathological, unwanted, and unnecessary. A psychopharmacologist or unsuspecting primary care physician trying to help a patient may vigorously attempt to obliterate the process, as might be done with delusions, hallucinations, or panic attacks. Short of dramatically compromising the patient's overall functioning through use of extreme amounts of medication, attempting cessation of dissociation will usually prove futile. More realistically, we try to modulate the dissociative process and quiet the extent of disruption it may cause.

A popular conceptualization among psychopharmacologists of the sexually abused is to categorize the symptoms of post-traumatic stress disorder into two general groupings. Similar to the way that criteria are designated for PTSD in the DSM, symptoms are seen as arising from neurophysiological hyperarousal and/or avoidance or inhibition. In fact, observing many patients over time shows them to shift from states of avoidance to hyperarousal and back, a bimodal model. Avoidance mechanisms include affective numbing, social avoidance, and depression-like symptomatology. Hyperarousal includes flashback experiences, insomnia, panic, and active dissociative events. Serotonin (a neurotransmitter) is thought to function as a modulator of hyperarousal. Implementation of this general bimodal model simplifies the task of pharmacologic intervention. Medications that calm autonomic hyperarousal or enhance the serotonergic systems of the brain would be the first choice of treatment; consistent with this hypothesis, many patients with abuse trauma reactions are medicated with antidepressants, tranquilizers, and seritonin-specific drugs such as trazodone (Desyrel), fluoxetine (Prozac), or clomipramine (Anafranil).

Heroic attempts at treating the effects of traumatic stress have been documented. For example, Kinzie and Leung (1989) have shown some success in combining tricyclic antidepressants with clonidine, an antihypertensive (also used in the treatment of opiate withdrawal) that inhibits the adrenergic system. Curiously, they found that the antidepressant effects were not improved, but sleep disorder, nightmares, and general intrusive symptoms were ameliorated. Note that their patients were Cambodian refugees, which may limit applicability to the case of sexual traumatization.

Fichtner and others (1990) present a case report of a patient with multiple personality disorder whose episodic violent outbursts were decreased and control over dissociative events was increased by stopping lithium, replacing it with carbamazepine (Tegretol), and maintaining the neuroleptic fluphenazine (Prolixin) at a dose of 5 mg twice daily. Serum levels of the carbamazepine were maintained near 8.0 microg/ml. Carbamazepine, generally used as an anticonvulsant, is thought to specifically effect limbic system structures, which are considered to be regions of affect and memory regulation. Their hypotheses were in agreement with those of Braun (1984) describing dissociation as a product of activation of structures in the limbic system of the brain in the context of state-dependent learning. On the other hand, Putnam (1988), in describing the pharmacology of multiple personality disorder, expresses little confidence in the use of anticonvulsants in the long term. In addition, he does mention that lithium may suppress switching of personalities, neuroleptics in his experience have no effect on dissociative symptoms, and antidepressants and anxiolytics (tranquilizers) should be used only when depression and anxiety manifest significantly in all alter personalities. The danger, according to Putnam, is that unnecessary medication may activate certain unwanted alters and suppress other more regulating, friendlier personalities.

To date, there is no known medication that can specifically halt the dissociative process, short of extreme sedation. This means we cannot predictably control dissociative process with medication (Fichtner et al. 1990; Friedman 1988). We can, however, attempt to control triggering phenomena and associated affective, anxiety, cognitive, and behavioral reactions.

Affective and Behavioral Dyscontrol

What follows is a discussion of some of the most troublesome and disturbing clinical phenomena for mental health practitioners, namely, patients losing emotional and behavioral control. In this grouping of symptoms are a broad range of complex behaviors and psychological experiences. The span includes emotional "storms" manifested as privately suffered despair and confusion, rituals of self-mutilation, and sudden verbal or violent outbursts, as well as more complicated "life-styles" of dyscontrol, such as eating disorders, substance abuse, promiscuity, and repeated self-destructive or abusive relationships.

The etiology of the dyscontrol of emotion and resulting behavioral loss of control is believed to lie in the effects of trauma on the central and autonomic nervous systems. According to Kolb (1987) and van der Kolk (1988), traumatic experiences lead to autonomic hyperarousal. The resulting effect is a lowered threshold to overstimulation and concomitant dyscontrol. Instances of major depression, hypomania, brief reactive psychosis, retraumatization, dissociative tendencies, and in particular, alcohol, caffeine, or other drug abuse, including that of prescribed medications (Gardner and Cowdry 1985; Soloff et al. 1986), are known to increase the possibility for dyscontrol.

Other experiences that may alter or surpass the stimulus threshold for affective and behavioral modulation include noise, music, sexual stimulation, disappointment, separation or perceived rejection by significant others, and in some patients, occasions where intense but possibly appropriate anger arises (as in an argument), significant changes in life experience, and successes such as promotion, graduation, performance, or completing a project. The effects of such experiences on triggering overstimulation and a dyscontrol reaction may vary in a given individual. In part, they are determined by the quality and availability of environmental supports. Also important to keep in mind when comparing individuals is that what may be unbearable for one person may call to action effective adaptive mechanisms in another.

Next to suicide attempts, perhaps the most disturbing of dyscontrol behaviors is patient self-mutilation. To simple observation, it is puzzling why someone who has suffered abuse by others would turn to injury at their own hands. Unfortunately, patients do harm themselves, apparently for different reasons. For example, some react impulsively to feeling overwhelmed or overstimulated, some seek the paradoxical tension relief after the act, and others feel unable to control their behavior whether or not they feel overwhelmed at the time.

There are neuropsychiatric theories of dyscontrol that address each of these three examples. The first, with Kolb and van der Kolk as its major proponents, was described above. In this theory, tendencies to become quickly overstimulated may lead to dyscontrol. Pharmacologic treatment would be directed at autonomic hyperarousal, which it is hoped would lead to diminished destructive overreactions. Some improvement with the use of propranolol in fairly high doses (160 mg or more daily) and clonidine has been reported (Kolb, Burris, and Griffiths 1984, Kinzie and Leung 1989). Unfortunately, there are the complications of toxic side effects such as altered cognitive functioning, depression, delirium, and hypotension. Tranquilizers, typically benzodiazepines, have been used commonly to diminish autonomic arousal. These are generally effective but have complications of oversedation, physiologic dependence (with dangerous withdrawal syndromes), amnesic reactions in high doses, and reported enhancement of behavioral dyscontrol in some patients taking alprazolam (Xanax; Gardner and Cowdry 1985) and lorazepam (Ativan; Little and Taghavi 1991), though similar reactions have been cited with essentially all benzodiazepines but oxazepam (Serax; Bond and Lader 1988). The associated dyscontrol appears to be dose dependent. With the shorter acting of these drugs, the dyscontrol may arise from increased irritability as the blood level of the medication drops, a kind of miniwithdrawal state. This could complicate the use of occasional doses in susceptible patients.

A second neuropsychiatric theory of self-mutilation refers to individuals who report tension relief and calm from self-injury. Bessel van der Kolk and others (1989) describe what they call "stress-induced analgesia" to account for this observation. They report how patients with post-traumatic stress disorder show an increase in physical pain tolerance, psychic numbing, and subjective tension reduction in response to a stress experience. Self-mutilation, if seen as a self-induced stress experience, generates a postinjury calm and numbing that may be gratifying to traumatized individuals. Self-injury then becomes a predictable means of achieving tension reduction that reinforces its own perpetuation.

Neurophysiologically, van der Kolk suggests this process is mediated by internal opiatelike substances. He and other researchers (see Winchel and Stanley 1991 for an excellent review of the subject) have shown preliminary results with certain patients (not sexually abused) that receptor blockade with opiate antagonists such as intravenous naloxone may temporarily diminish self-mutilation. In theory, use of an orally administered opiate antagonist such as naltrexone may lessen the experience of gratification from the opiate response to self-injury in trauma victims. The hope is that without the subjective reinforcer of tension relief, the frequency of the behavior would decrease. To date, there are no published reports of naltrexone trials with self-injurious sexually abused individuals. Hence, its use for this purpose would be considered purely experimental.

The third neuropsychiatric theory has been presented in the literature by Gardner and Cowdry (1985, 1986). These authors have supported their hypotheses by citing the results of their research of medication trials with self-mutilating patients meeting diagnostic criteria for borderline personality disorder. They did not study sexually abused individuals specifically; however, their findings have applicability here. The foundation of their hypothesis is the similarity of symptoms of patients with complex partial seizures and borderline personality disorder. The authors emphasize dysfunction in the limbic structures of the brain that generate human emotional experience and influence emotion-related behaviors and memories. The theory suggests the etiology of behavioral dyscontrol as a mechanism that involves "epileptoid overactivity of limbic structures" (Gardner and Cowdry 1986).

Gardner and Cowdry studied a sample of eleven females with significant histories of behavioral dyscontrol, including suicidal action, self-mutilation, and rage attacks. They suggested that the pharmacologic treatment of choice, given their theory, would be an anticonvulsant with specific effects on the limbic system—that is, carbamazepine (Tegretol). Their findings showed a significant decrease in the severity of self-destructive behaviors of dyscontrol in the women taking carbamazepine. It appears this may be a useful drug in helping some patients control acting-out behavior; unfortunately, it is not an easy medication to take. Frequent blood testing is necessary because of potentially hazardous side effects on the bone marrow and liver. Also, skin rashes and lightheadedness are common. Lithium carbonate, divalproex sodium (Depakote), and clonazepam (Klonopin), a long-acting benzodiazepine and anticonvulsant, may also be helpful as alternatives.

The three theoretical approaches described are on equal grounds. It should be understood that there is no evidence that any of them deserves predominance. To be sure, a pharmacological approach based in any one of the hypotheses will not suffice to diminish dyscontrol in even a majority of cases. Diagnostically, the challenge before us is to attempt to distinguish differences in our patients that could guide our treatment decisions regardless of theoretical belief. But even within the confines of the three described hypotheses, it would be most useful if we could find a way to distinguish individuals with hyperarousal problems and low stimulus thresholds for behavioral dyscontrol predictably from those who mutilate to self-soothe and from those that show a more episodic, less predictable type of dyscontrol. Clinical presentations, however, are rarely so clear.

To summarize this section on affective and behavioral dyscontrol, pharmacologic intervention should be recommended only after psychotherapeutic, cognitive (for example, keeping a journal as in treatment of bulimia), and interpersonal (social contact when at risk) treatment attempts have clearly failed. None of the available medications are clearly effective, and all of them carry potentially serious risks. Of course, these suggestions stand only if the patient's threshold for dyscontrol is not altered by a major psychiatric disorder such as depression, mania, psychosis, or severe forms of anxiety disorder.

The Problem of Multisymptom Presentation

Few clinicians have difficulty in recognizing such major psychopathology as agoraphobia, depression, or psychosis. The task becomes problematic when patients present with multiple symptoms and concurrent disability in describing their symptoms clearly and accurately. Patients commonly sent to pharmacologists for consultation show a mix of anxiety symptoms, depressive features, dissociative tendencies, confusional states, racing thoughts, and suicidal ideation. Where does one begin? How does one prioritize treatment?

First, it is assumed that the psychodynamic and psychosocial factors mentioned early in this chapter have been given adequate forethought. Secondly, it is assumed that time has been spent with the referring therapist to obtain as much relevant psychological and social history as possible. Third, with the patient before you, adequate consideration must be given to developing a workable treatment relationship. It is not uncommon, particularly with male physicians seeing high-functioning female patients with histories of abuse, that very early on in the consultation patients may comment or complain regarding the clinician's attitude, demeanor, appearance, or choice of questions. This kind of behavior on the part of patients should be respected as necessary to the process of developing a "safe" relationship with the male psychiatrist. Debate or dialogue with the patient about details or distortions beyond fundamental clarifications are typically unessential and could further complicate an already sensitive experience. Fourth, a detailed history of the patient's difficulties should be obtained, including ongoing exploration of the patient's wishes, expectations, and fears regarding your consultation and potential interventions.

At this point in the evaluation, a not-to-be-missed question must be addressed: whether the patient is in crisis, out of control, or dangerous in any way. Next, one needs to rule out significant substance use or chemical dependency. Depending on the circumstances, these issues (if present) are priority conditions and typically require specific intervention and planning. It is highly recommended that addressing dangerousness and chemical use be integrally woven into the ongoing clinical assessment of abuse victims.

As the evaluation proceeds, the pharmacologist then tries to determine the presence or absence of medication-responsive primary major psychiatric illness. The list of "rule-outs" would include primary severe anxiety disorders (including a general state of hyperarousal or overstimulation), affective disorders, psychotic disorders, and disorders of impulse and dyscontrol. Each of these have specific pharmacologic interventions known to be useful in symptom management.

After primary psychiatric syndromes are given consideration, secondary phenomena are evaluated. Most commonly seen are symptoms of anxiety, irritability, insomnia, occasional panic, dysphoria, episodic despair, dissociative experiences, self-injury and abreactive dyscontrol. In the absence of clear-cut primary psychopathology, pharmacologic treatment of secondary symptomatology is purely a matter of judgment. If the psychiatrist keeps in mind how responsive all the symptoms mentioned are to psychosocial interventions, he or she will not feel compelled to prescribe. Again, the evaluation of psychological and environmental supports may be more important in arriving at the decision to medicate or not than individual patient-based medical psychiatric assessment.

Diagnostic skills to hone include the ability to distinguish agitation from hypomania, psychosis from dissociation, other forms of dyscontrol, and abreaction. A major complication in evaluation lies in the fact that many (if not all) abused patients experience periods of abreaction as part of the recuperative process. This abreaction can vary dramatically in appearance and duration, mimicking manipulative regressions of borderline states, lethal crises, and psychotic reactions. One quickly discovers that treating abreaction pharmacologically is often futile and requires dramatic amounts of sedation. Here, psychosocial intervention (if possible), hospitalization (if completely unavoidable), and sedation (if absolutely necessary to safeguard physical health) are the treatments of choice.

It deserves repeating that for unknown reasons, the symptomatology of abuse victims may not respond to medication as predicted, and side effect profiles may be somewhat unusual. For example, it would not be uncommon to see antidepressant effects from low-dose regimens of neuroleptics, sedation and fatigue from fluoxetine (Prozac) and bupropion (Wellbutrin), agitation from typically sedating tricyclic antidepressants such as imipramine (Tofranil) and amitriptyline (Elavil), more dramatic behavioral disinhibition than expected from lorazepam (Ativan) and other benzodiazepines, and increased memory deficits from benzodiazepines and benztropine (Cogentin).

In closing this chapter on the pharmacologic treatment of the complicated clinical states of sexually abused patients, a bit of professional reality testing is in order. Our knowledge as psychopharmacologists of how to treat the complex reactions of sexual abuse with specificity is essentially primitive. On a more optimistic note, researchers are actively looking for general unifying theories and approaches to simplify the clinical process. Also, clinicians are studying their patients diligently to find familiar or repeating patterns of symptoms to guide their clinical decisions. Unfortunately, even when skilled psychopharmacologists follow thoughtfully considered indications, uncomfortable and at times catastrophic side effects are the result.

The use of psychiatric medications in treating complex abuse reactions in these times primarily serves an adjunctive role to careful psychotherapy and rehabilitation treatment planning. The task set before the contemporary psychiatrist is to avoid unnecessary prescription, overmedication, or even worse, psychotherapeutic interference.

References

Asaad, G. (1990). *Hallucinations in Clinical Psychiatry: A Guide for Mental Health Professionals.* New York: Brunner/Mazel.

Bond, A., & Lader, M. (1988). Differential effects of oxazepam and lorazepam on aggressive responding. *Psychopharmacology* 95:369–73.

Braun, B. G. (1984). Towards a theory of multiple personality and other dissociative phenomena. *Psychiatric Clinics of North America* 7: 171–93.

Davidson, J., Kudler, H., Smith, R., Mahorney, S. L., Lipper, S., Hammett, E., Saunders, W. B., & Cavenar, J. O. (1990). Treatment of posttraumatic stress disorder with amitriptyline and placebo. *Archives of General Psychiatry* 47:259–66.

Fichtner, C. G., Kuhlman, D. T., Gruenfeld, M. J., & Hughes, J. R. (1990). Decreased episodic violence and increased control of dissociation in a carbamazepine treated case of multiple personality. *Biological Psychiatry* 27:1045–52.

Friedman, M. (1988). Toward rational pharmacotherapy for posttraumatic stress disorder: an interim report. *American Journal of Psychiatry* 145:281–85.

Gardner, D. L., and Cowdry, R. W. (1985). Alprazolam-induced dyscontrol in borderline personality disorder. *American Journal of Psychiatry* 142:98–100.

Gardner, D. L., and Cowdry, R. W. (1986). Positive effects of carbamazepine on behavioral dyscontrol in borderline personality disorder. *American Journal of Psychiatry* 143:519–22.

Gunderson, J. G. (1984). *Borderline Personality Disorder.* Washington, DC: American Psychiatric Press.

Gut, E. (1989). *Productive and Unproductive Depression.* New York: Basic Books.

Kinzie, J. D., and Leung, P. (1989). Clonidine in Cambodian patients with posttraumatic stress disorder. *Journal of Nervous and Mental Disease* 177:546–50.

Kolb, L. C., Burris, B. C., Griffiths, S. (1984). Propranolol and clonidine in the treatment of posttraumatic stress of war. In B. P. van der Kolk (Ed.), *Traumatic Stress Disorders: Psychological and Biological Sequelae.* Washington, DC: American Psychiatric Press, pp. 29–42.

Kolb, L. C. (1987). Neuropsychological hypothesis explaining post-traumatic stress disorder. *American Journal of Psychiatry* 144:989–95.

Lerer, B., Avraham, B., Kotler, M., Garb, R., Hertzberg, M., & Levin, B. (1987). Posttraumatic stress disorder in Israeli combat veterans. *Archives of General Psychiatry* 44:976–81.

Little, J. D., & Taghavi, E. H. (1991). Disinhibition after lorazepam augmentation of antipsychotic medication. *American Journal of Psychiatry* 148:1099.

Ludwig, A. M. (1983). The psychobiological functions of dissociation. *American Journal of Clinical Hypnosis* 26:93–99.

Putnam, F. W. (1988). *Diagnosis and Treatment of Multiple Personality Disorder.* New York: Guilford Press.

Roose, S. P., & Glassman, A. H. (1990). Treatment Strategies for Refractory Depression. Washington, D.C.: American Psychiatric Press.

Ross, C. A., Shaun, J., Currie, R. (1990). Dissociative experiences in the general population. *American Journal of Psychiatry* 147:1547–52.

Soloff, P. H., George, A., Nathan, S., Schulz, P. M., Ulrich, R. F., Paul, J. M. (1986). Progress in pharmacotherapy of borderline disorders. *Archives of General Psychiatry* 43:691–97.

Tobin, D. L., and Johnson, C. L. (1991). The integration of psychodynamic and behavioral therapy in the treatment of eating disorders: clinical issues versus theoretical mystique. In C. L. Johnson (Ed.), *Psychodynamic Treatment of Anorexia Nervosa and Bulimia* New York: Guilford Press, pp. 374–397.

van der Kolk, B. A. (Ed.). (1984). *Post-Traumatic Stress Disorder: Psycho-*

logical and Biological Sequelae. Washington, DC: American Psychiatric Press.

van der Kolk, B. A. (1987). The drug treatment of post-traumatic stress disorder. *Journal of Affective Disorders 13*:203–13.

van der Kolk, B. A. (1988). The trauma spectrum: The interaction of biological and social events in the genesis of the trauma response. *Journal of Traumatic Stress 1*:273–90.

van der Kolk, B. A., Greenberg, M. S., Orr, S. P., & Pitman, R. K. (1989). Endogenous opioids, stress induced analgesia, and posttraumatic stress disorder. *Psychopharmacology Bulletin 25*:417–21.

van der Kolk, B. A., & van der Hart, O. (1989). Pierre Janet and the breakdown or adaptation in psychological trauma. *American Journal of Psychiatry 146*:1530–40.

Winchel, R. M., & Stanley, M. (1991). Self-injurious behavior: A review of the behavior and biology of self-mutilation. *American Journal of Psychiatry 148*:306–17.

6

Diverse Presentations of Substance Abuse and Post-traumatic Stress Disorder in Incest Survivors

Barbara G. Orrok

Introduction

Incest, Substance Abuse, and
Post-traumatic Stress Disorder

A connection between incest and substance abuse is undisputed: substance abuse is a common problem for incest survivors (Schetky 1990). Practitioners making a specialty in the treatment of one of these problems, however, often are unfamiliar with the other, despite recognizing that they are frequently intertwined (Nace 1988). The dynamic psychotherapist may find interpretive work inadequate to treat substance abuse. Similarly, the substance abuse counselor often is unfamiliar with techniques beyond the immediate management of sobriety and may thus be unequipped to treat trauma victims.

Increasingly sophisticated studies show that incest is more prevalent than epidemiologists and mental health workers had imagined (Russell 1986; Browne and Finklehor 1986). Workers in the field have had to cope with facing this fact and then trying to convince colleagues of what appears to be an ongoing epidemic. Resistance to recognition of the widespread existence of incest has dogged most workers in the field; some have gone largely unnoticed (Weinstein 1955). Some have been plagued by doubt, perhaps swayed by their own and colleagues' disbelief and distaste. Perhaps the most widely quoted case of confusion about the prevalence of incest is that of Freud. Initially, he appeared convinced that incest was at the root of his patients' hysterical symptoms, but later he recanted in favor of fantasied incestuous relations (Freud [1933] 1955).

113

There has been some debate over the traumatic aspects of incest (Benedek 1984; Russell 1986). It is not the purpose of this chapter to review this debate. Rather, this chapter assumes that incestuous relations are traumatic and that a number of incest victims go on to experience sequelae of trauma, some of which are easily recognized. There are also other, more subtle sequelae, however, that mislead patients and their clinicians (Gelinas 1983). Among these sequelae is substance abuse; in addition, post-traumatic stress disorder (PTSD) appears to exist in many incest survivors (Gelinas 1983; Donaldson and Gardner 1985; Lindberg and Distad 1985). Treatment of PTSD is often confined to veterans' centers and may be unfamiliar to dynamic, behavioral, and substance abuse clinicians who have not worked with veterans. Often, neither therapists specializing in incest nor incest victims themselves are familiar with the interconnections between substance abuse and post-traumatic problems. The outcome of this knowledge deficit is often reflected in fragmented or incomplete treatment. For these patients and therapists, their multiple problems may never be satisfactorily integrated into a global view that relates how each problem augments the others and how together they confound recovery. Increased comfort with both substance abuse and PTSD can increase the clinician's index of suspicion in the recognition and successful treatment of incest victims.

Recent research in biological psychiatry has started to illuminate neurochemical connections between trauma and substance abuse. Although this research is in the earliest phases, it gives hope for an explanation of why substance use is so frequently employed as a coping mechanism by trauma victims. It is tempting to stretch these early findings to create biological correlates for psychodynamic and behavioral constructs.

Different Presentations and Different Models

Each case of incest is different, although all have in common the violation of sexual boundaries by family members. Incest survivors have displayed every known outcome from complete social and psychological decompensation to great creativity and success. Sexual relationships between a parent and prepubescent child necessarily have different implications for perpetrator and victim than those between siblings close in age. Differences in the nature and degree of pathology in the perpetrator as well as in the ego strength of the victim contribute to the nature of the incestuous relationship and its outcome. There may also be biochemical factors that contribute to different outcomes, and these may turn out to be reflections of genetic makeup or may be environmentally stimulated.

For many reasons, victims may not reveal their incest experiences until well into a course of therapy, if at all. It is not uncommon that incest survivors do not remember the incest or do not believe it to be the source of their problems when they present for treatment. They may withhold the history for fear of alienating the therapist or fear of revenge by the perpetrator (Goodwin 1985). More common are chief complaints that include listlessness, alienation, dysphoria, anxiety, inability to maintain meaningful long-term relationships, sleep disturbance, nightmares, anger, conduct disorders or behavioral problems, sexual dysfunction, or substance abuse (Briere and Runtz 1988; Donaldson and Gardner 1985). Often, patient and therapist are confused by the apparently unrelated symptoms or the apparent lack of evidence of a dynamic etiology for them. Once a history of incest is revealed, diverse and apparently unrelated symptoms and concerns often fall into place. Treatment can then proceed in a more orderly fashion. In some cases, making the diagnosis of PTSD may enable the clinician to suspect incest or other childhood abuse, which may clear the way for the patient to reflect on a past that was previously too dangerous to recall.

Once the incest is revealed, individualized psychodynamic formulations can be made. These may involve the nature of the symptoms, the relationship of perpetrator and victim, the victim's individual psychological makeup, and the resultant meanings of the trauma. Dynamic formulations can be supplemented by the more generalized and growing body of knowledge regarding PTSD; behavioral strategies and/or medications might be considered. Moving from the specific situation of incest to the wider category of PTSD may also provide clinician and patient with broader paradigms with which to understand the trauma and the patient's reactions to it. Many clinicians and patients find it helpful to use a psychoeducational approach: defining a syndrome makes the presenting symptoms more predictable and less unique, bizarre, or overwhelming.

Goals

This chapter will review and combine some concepts and constructs pulled from the areas of substance abuse, incest, trauma, family systems analysis, learning theory, and biological psychiatry to illustrate how these approaches augment each other to improve our understanding and treatment of incest. Appropriately disguised vignettes are presented that clinicians will probably find familiar from their own caseloads. The goal of this chapter is to orient clinicians to some of the complexities involved in assessing the incest survivor for other psychological problems or, more commonly, assessing substance abusers for incest. Increasingly accurate diagnosis and expanded theoretical knowledge may contribute to the clinician's ability to forge meaningful therapeutic relationships with patients. There is no unifying theory of substance abuse and post-traumatic stress disorder as specific sequelae of incest at this time, and the evidence seems to be getting more rather than less complex. Although the theories presented here are highly speculative, they suggest possibilities for the understanding and treatment of incest survivors.

The following sections use cases to illustrate some commonly observed relationships among incest, substance abuse, and post-traumatic stress disorder. First, substance abuse will be examined in the context of the family. Roles and relationships within the addictive family shift to accommodate the addict's decreasing level of function while preserving the family unit. These pathologic shifts can set the stage for incest as roles are reversed and other boundaries are transgressed. The case orientation should alert clinicians to consider the possibility that incest can exist in the "ordinary" addictive family.

Post-traumatic stress disorder will then be reviewed with special attention to substance abuse and incest. All too often, patients' symptoms do not fall easily into place, especially if the trauma is not revealed, and the clinician must be alert to what is usually a fragmentary presentation of PTSD.

Finally, several theoretical models relating substance abuse and PTSD will be outlined, with inferences to the situation of incest as the underlying trauma. Each model has strengths explaining different aspects of these problems. At this time, no single model provides a unifying model of the psychological and physiological sequelae of incest. The case material presented in the subsequent sections will be recalled to illustrate how the various models may be helpful in different clinical situations that might be encountered in office practice.

Substance Abuse in Family Systems

Substance abuse can cause or intensify any family problem. One well-recognized problem is the loss of function of the impaired family member, leading to overcompensation by another family member in order for the family to survive. A second problem is blurring of boundaries with loss of impulse control, which can lead to the transgression of boundaries. Parentification of children; verbal, emotional, and physical abuse; and incest are common examples of boundary violations.

A third problem arises as a paradox: the family's attempts to correct the substance abuse may actually reinforce it. Taking a stance that one family member can stop the drug use of another forms the core of an oppositional relationship. The identified family member approaches the addict and outlines the problem. Often this alienates the substance abuser, who can then focus on the discomfort of the confrontation rather than on stopping the substance abuse. Defensive attitudes such as, "Hey, my drinking isn't hurting anyone; what's your problem?" parallel the strategies of projective identification (Ogden 1979). In this situation, the addict continues to deny the severity of the substance abuse while focusing on the family member's distress, which is actually caused by the addict's own behaviors.

Another facet of this paradoxical response can be explained by the principles of operant conditioning (Skinner 1953), which also can explain some facets of this sequence of events in the family system. Families cover up for the addict who misses work, and so forth. The family is then protected from outside scrutiny and from punishment (such as loss of the addict's income). At the same time, the addict is released from these deserved negative consequences of the substance abuse. At this point, the addictive behaviors have been rewarded or reinforced, and abstinent behaviors have not. As other family members take up the addict's family responsibilities, the addict becomes extruded and may remain so during abstinent periods. For example, if the addict cannot be relied upon to make decisions about child rearing when intoxicated, the family member who becomes responsible for these decisions is likely to continue at this task during the addict's abstinent periods as the family loses faith in the addict. In this case, the abstinent behavior is not reinforced. Attempts to address irresponsible behaviors until the addict is sober enough for a discussion are a sensible plan, as few problems can be solved while the addict is intoxicated. This increases the likelihood, however, that sober periods will be more unpleasant than intoxicated episodes. Thus, the addictive behavior is reinforced and the abstinent behavior punished. Not receiving positive reinforcement for abstinence while perceiving disdain/extrusion/punishment in general, and during abstinent periods in particular, sets the stage for relapse to substance abuse and other accompanying dysfunctional behaviors. Thus, the family's attempts to cope with the addict can unintentionally create a situation in which the addict finds no incentive to abstain (Leonard 1990).

Characteristics of incestuous families are similar to those of alcoholic families (Courtois 1988; Bepko and Krestan 1985). Some of these include collective denial and shared secrets about problems in addition to the incest, duplicity, and deceit between family members, which develop into protective family myths, social isolation, denial of obvious family problems, role confusion and boundary diffusion, triangulation of a child into the parents' marriage, poor tolerance for anger, conflict and differences from family norms, high overt moral standards, and inadequate and intermittent responsibility shown toward child rearing and violence (Calof 1988).

Substance abuse is often accompanied by a multitude of the problems in the family. When a family presents with substance abuse, incest should be in the clinician's differential. Incest perpetrators frequently are substance abusers. Victims often turn to substance abuse, which may be initiated by the perpetrator and may help the victim tolerate the sexual activity. Often, trauma victims report that substance abuse numbs the traumatic memories (Root 1989). As will be discussed later, however, the use of alcohol and drugs to quell memories may actually lead to their exacerbation.

Powerful emotions, including guilt, shame, and rage, can become dominant when families attempt to cope with problems such as substance abuse or incest. Scapegoating or extrusion of a family member may provide a temporary sense of relief. Projection, projective identification, splitting, and denial may be employed. These may be used between members but also may be used by the family for protection from outside forces. Even when stressed, threatened with discovery, or faced with the loss of a family member, the family may close ranks as a last attempt to avoid society's devastating judgment.

The following vignettes illustrate some pathologic patterns found in families with substance abuse and incest.

Reassignment of Roles

A case example: J. was a fifteen-year-old who presented with a clergywoman to a private practitioner for help. J. had been increasingly despondent during her weekly church duties, and gradually the cleric gained her confidence. Together, they recounted J.'s increasing distress, which started in family therapy at the local clinic. Family therapy had been recommended after her brother, T., was arrested for driving while intoxicated.

T. was a seventeen-year-old referred to treatment by the legal system's alternative program for minors. He presented to the local clinic as a swaggering young man who employed a devil-may-care attitude to hide his distress at his life being out of control. Over the preceding year and a half, he had become increasingly involved with a group of peers who drank heavily on weekends and at social occasions. They were suspected in a number of incidents of vandalism. As work began, it became clear that his family was greatly distressed by T.'s arrest, feeling publicly shamed. They agreed to come for an interview, which revealed T.'s father to be loudly critical of his son, his mother at her "wits' end," and his sister, J., quietly embarrassed by the three of them. There seemed to be some family consensus that if only T. would straighten up, the family would be perfect.

Family therapy was initiated, with the goal of averting the developing process of extruding T. from the family. Engaging the family was difficult, presumably because they did not want to reveal family secrets. These included the father's chronic drinking, the mother's chronic anger, and J.'s developing depression and dropping grades. As the father drank more, family finances were strained. The mother had taken on a part-time job in addition to trying to manage the family's finances. J.'s role had been that of the perfect and parentified child, helping with chores and trying to keep the peace. It began to appear as if T.'s brazen disobedience was developing as an attempt to divert family attention from his sister's depression. When attention was turned to her, she stopped coming to sessions, giving various excuses.

J. had been somewhat relieved at the interest shown by the cleric, and she had slowly begun to tell her own story. Her brother and father had been molesting her for some time. Years ago, her father had begun sexual relations with her, threatening her if she were to tell. Over the last six months, her brother had discovered their secret and had blackmailed her into allowing him sexual favors as well. She did not know whether her father was aware of this, and she felt mortified and abandoned by her family. The chaplain felt these problems required more than spiritual guidance and had come with J. to support her through her ordeal.

The family had not revealed this in their treatment, and J. was too frightened and ashamed to bring it up in the sessions, so she had dropped out.

A family systems approach has been applied to the alcoholic family (Bennett and Wolin 1990) and can probably reasonably be applied to other addictive families as well. This model postulates that the family is an organizational unit that is affected by the alcoholism and that helps maintain continued drinking. Alcoholism may stabilize the family, even if in an unhealthy state of equilibrium. In this case, the symptoms of the identified patient (the son) express the family's disturbance while protecting the rest of the family from scrutiny. Family communications reinforce the family's denial of the existence of other problems. Family boundaries tend to be rigid/impermeable, leading to isolation of the family from the outside world (Steinglass 1982). Rigid boundaries against the outside are seen in other examples as well.

Although the substance abuse history was accessible, the family seemed willing to sacrifice the son to keep the incest secret. Family therapy was proceeding without the therapist being aware of the incest. Often, adolescent drinking is predictive of other problems—not only of use of other illicit drugs, but also of antisocial behavior (Barnes 1990). If we are to accept modeling and socialization as important factors in the development of family patterns of substance abuse (Marlatt 1985), it seems a short leap of faith to consider these influences as affecting the development of attitudes toward sexuality.

As the substance abuser becomes dysfunctional, other family members take on the abandoned functions in order to keep the family going. Thus, chores, administrative functions and even intimate relationships are redistributed. Parental sexual intimacy may be disturbed by the substance abuse, for reasons such as increased arousal, accompanied by decreased male sexual performance, as direct sequelae of alcohol use. Often, however, substance abuse is not the sole cause of marital dysfunction. Conflict in the marital dyad can lead to an equal level of sexual dysfunction. In addictive families, conflictual as well as physiologic causes of sexual dysfunction may result from the substance abuse (O'Farrell 1990).

Not all adjustments to substance abuse are perceived as undesirable. The spouse/parent who abandons executive function as the addiction progresses leaves an opening for the other spouse or adolescent child to develop skills to maintain money management, create and enforce family rules, and arrange family vacations. The spouse/

parent who abdicates domestic function creates a place for a grandparent or other adult relative to raise the children, provide a nurtur-
ing environment, develop family rituals, and be a central figure in
family life. Complementary patterns of over- and underresponsibility
develop together. Often the family members who have been enlisted
to perform these functions enjoy them (even if ambivalently), are
proud of being able to take over these important tasks, and do not
give them up easily. Sometimes, problematic behaviors such as incest
create desirable roles, such as intimacy or overidentification between
family members. Inertia as well as fear of change are compounded
with enjoyment of the adjusted family roles to keep the family stable,
albeit unhealthy. This stability resists change. *Enabling* is that part
of resistance that involves the overcompensation of other family
members so that the addict continues substance abuse and does not
regain access to appropriate family roles (Wegscheider 1981; Bepko
and Krestan 1985).

Substance abusers may be ambivalent about their roles being
taken over by other members. Interest in maintaining age- and role-
appropriate behavior may wane, and perception of self may be distorted due to continued substance abuse (Bepko and Krestan 1985).
These may favor relief at the decline in function. On the other hand,
few people can remain completely oblivious to the loss of their place
in the family or to the distress of other family members in this process. Those who feel the loss and distress but are unequipped to confront them head-on may attempt to deal with the disturbing affect in
maladaptive ways. Flirtation and seduction may go beyond a need
to replace the spouse's lost affection; they may become the addict's
weapon against a spouse who is experienced as usurping the addict's
place in the family. The spouse, alienated by the troubles brought on
by the addiction, may overlook the incest because it cancels the need
to be intimate with the addict.

Another circumstance involving reassignment of roles that appears to increase the risk of father-daughter incest is absence of the
mother due to illness or other disability (such as substance abuse,
separation, or death). The mother's role is then left open, possibly to
be filled by a daughter (Herman and Hirschman 1981).

Re-establishment of Stability

A case example: M. was a twenty-five-year-old college graduate
working successfully as a bank's junior vice president. She presented

for psychotherapy on referral from her gynecologist, to whom she had complained of frigidity in the face of her upcoming marriage. She felt she loved and trusted her fiancé, but she was unable to respond to his intimate advances unless she was "loosened up" with a drink or some marijuana. This was all the more bothersome to her because her father, dead for some years, was alcoholic. She feared that she, too, might be on the road to troublesome drinking.

As the therapy progressed, M. developed a sense of foreboding and put the marriage off for an indefinite period. Gradually, she recalled increasing details of her relationship with her father. Eventually this included a period during her early adolescence in which her father, drunk, had sexual relations with her in her room at night when the rest of the family was asleep.

Even if this woman's father had been alive, it would have been impossible to tell whether he drank to decrease his inhibitions about molesting his daughter, whether his drinking brought on the idea, or whether he had any recollection of what he had done (that is, whether he was in alcohol-induced blackouts during these episodes).

M.'s lifelong patterns of achievement may be an example of the stabilizing roles taken on by family members, and sometimes friends, of alcoholics. Stabilizing roles commonly taken on by children in alcoholic (and probably other addictive) families include the hero, the scapegoat, and the mascot (Wegscheider 1981). The *hero* responds to the family's distress by trying to achieve successes that can correct the family's weaknesses, and to distract from the painful realities of the substance abuse. M.'s good behavior may have made her the family's hero, and as such, she may have felt special as the father's chosen object, or disloyal if she believed or reported the aggression of his sexual advances. These factors may have stabilized the family unit even though they contributed to her subsequent discomfort with intimacy.

Briefly, some of the other children's stabilizing roles appear to function by drawing attention from the impaired parent to themselves. The *scapegoat,* the irresponsible child who draws attention away from the addicted parent with serious problems such as truancy, running away, and substance abuse, engages the family in a combative format. J.'s older brother, in the previous example, may be an example of a scapegoat. The *mascot's* ongoing immature, overactive antics also divert the family's attention—sometimes because of the mascot's developing school problems, hyperactivity, and so forth, and sometimes almost as comic relief as the family struggles to clean up after the messes the mascot leaves behind. As with the hero, these roles draw attention away from the addict and from the family stress caused by the addiction, but at the price of the child's healthy development. There is no evidence that any one type of these or other family stabilizers is prone to being the incest victim.

Alcohol or drugs themselves may become imbued with importance as family stabilizers. Being intoxicated may excuse inappropriate behavior so that the offending family member need not be chastised. Drinking may facilitate a relationship, often inappropriate, between two family members, such as the perpetrator who drinks in order to commit incest or the victim who drinks to tolerate it. In the case above, the habit of drinking to tolerate sexual contact emerged in adulthood, even after the memory of incest had been repressed.

Secrecy

A case example: G. was a bright sixteen-year-old who was sought out by the school counselor because of falling grades and social withdrawal. She was able to reveal that these changes had begun after her mother's boyfriend had moved in. The mother and boyfriend could not be pinned down to a specific appointment time. The following year, G. became psychotic, with prominent phallic delusions. She was hospitalized, which permitted a family evaluation. This revealed drug use and ritual sexual activity involving the mother's boyfriend and G. These behaviors had become so entrenched in the household that G. had been frightened to invite friends over, for fear that they would also be subject to these rituals.

Often, family attempts at secrecy appear to begin as attempts to preserve the family. For example, a family member will make excuses for an intoxicated or hung-over member. Gradually, family patterns develop to compensate for the addict's decreased participation in functional family activities (Leonard 1990). Mounting problems in the family often lead to a perceived need for the family to extrude outsiders (Steinglass 1982). Increasingly bizarre or inappropriate behaviors may be accepted or perpetuated within the family home, even with the tacit understanding that they are unacceptable to society and therefore must be kept secret. The onset of an incestuous relationship, which may have begun on the basis of intoxication decreasing the perpetrator's inhibitions, may become the greatest secret of all. Secrecy is an important contributing factor to the development of a sense of shame or isolation, which often becomes part of each family member's psyche. Recognizing family secrets and helping the family overcome the fear and shame of revealing and solving them are routine in family and family-oriented therapy. The therapist may be faced with the task of guessing the secret in order to help guide the family safely toward working on it. Therapists who keep a high index of suspicion about substance abuse may need to work consciously on developing a paired, equally high index for sexual abuse, and vice versa.

Regression and Other Undesirable Behavior Patterns

A case example: N. was a four-year-old girl brought by her divorced mother to her pediatrician for a return to bed-wetting; she had been toilet trained for well over a year. There seemed to be no physical etiology for the eneuresis. With further questioning, the pediatrician elicited the history that there were some other mild signs of regression, such as N.'s fear to be alone in her room at night. These problems had begun several weeks after N. had returned from a month with her maternal grandparents while her mother was in a drug and alcohol rehabilitation program. The doctor and mother decided that N. was reacting to having been separated from her home, and resolved to prepare her more thoroughly should any other separations be planned in the future.

Later in the mother's ongoing outpatient treatment for substance abuse, she recalled incestuous experiences with her own father. While working on the relationship between the incest and her drinking, she began to suspect that her daughter had regressed after being abused by her father (her daughter's grandfather) during that month spent with him.

Incest victims and children of substance abusers may have difficulty with developmental tasks (as did N.) or with forming or maintaining intimate relationships (as did her mother, or the successful M. in the earlier vignette). Other problems include school difficulties, legal problems, and the development of addictions. Positive human qualities such as basic trust, independence, and reliability may be stunted (Gelinas 1983; Meiselman 1981; Deutsche 1982). This problem may be caused both by boundary transgressions and by inadequate parental development, which leave the child without appropriate expectations or guidance. The behavior of the teenager T. earlier illustrates the development of undesirable behavior patterns. Secrecy, withdrawal, or violence may develop in part because of modeling (behavioral imitation of parental behavior patterns) or because of inadequate development of self-esteem (dynamic developmental patterns.) When incest occurs, these patterns gain stronger rigidity.

An additional risk factor is posed in this case: the child of a single mother may be exposed to fluid family constellations with poorly defined family boundaries. In families where one parent is alcoholic (and probably the same holds true with other addictions), divorce is frequent when the mother is the addict; the marriage is more likely to stay intact when the father is the sole addict. As noted above, a father's alcoholism poses its own challenges to intergenerational boundaries. When the mother is impaired and is single, the likelihood of multiple male temporary partners is increased, and boundaries prohibiting sexual relationships with children are weaker than in ongoing biologic families. Similarly, a recombined family in which the oldest daughter is from a previous liason and is separated by many years from the couple's shared children is also at risk for sexual and other abuse.

These cases have described a few of the many presentations of incest and substance abuse using family systems constructs. From the systems perspective, substance abuse may be significant in either the perpetrator or the victim. The next section will focus on the traumatic paradigm. In this paradigm, both incest and its sequela, substance abuse, have post-traumatic implications for the victim.

Post-traumatic Stress Disorder (PTSD)

Over the years, attention has focused on characterizing specific syndromes experienced by trauma victims (Trimble 1985); A definitive description is still evolving. Most workers agree that PTSD includes a combination of physical and emotional symptoms and does not develop equally in all trauma survivors. Much of the work characterizing PTSD has been done on veterans but appears equally applicable to other traumatized persons as well, including incest victims (Wilson, Smith, and Johnson 1985).

After the traumatic experience, the victim who goes on to PTSD develops new symptoms that persist over an extended period of time. These troublesome episodes include periods in which the event is persistently reexperienced, either as intrusive memories or as nightmares. Stimuli associated with the event are avoided, consciously or unconsciously. Psychic numbing occurs, and increased physiologic arousal persists. All of these changes may occur immediately after the trauma or may not appear until a lengthy period of time has elapsed. They may appear spontaneously or in times of life stress. (American Psychiatric Association [APA] 1987)

Persistent Reexperience

A case example: P. was a twenty-two-year-old college senior in his second year of treatment for alcoholism at his college counseling service. In the spring semester, he became increasingly anxious about what job he would find and where he would live after graduation. He complained of disturbed sleep, with nightmares that he could not remember on awakening. He returned to drinking after being sober for well over a year, stating that it was the only way he could get to sleep. At first, his counselor interpreted this as a variant of expectable pregraduation jitters, and worked with P. to stop drinking and reinvolve himself with AA.

P. had entered treatment when he was a twenty-one-year-old college junior. He had been brought to the emergency room in an agitated and intoxicated state by his fraternity brothers, who reported that P. had become very drunk during a keg party. He had started to shout unintelligibly, then had become frightened of something that clearly was not in the room and had attempted to take cover under the table. The fraternity members admitted that P. was one of the heavier drinkers in the frat and did get wild when drunk from time to time, though they had never seen it this bad. They noted he was always amnesic for these episodes when they teased him afterward. P. was held for observation and released with a strong recommendation to report for treatment for his alcohol abuse. He had done this and was supported by his fraternity brothers. This relapse worried him; he began talking with his fraternity brothers at great length about his drinking habits in an attempt to understand the relapse. Then, in a counseling session, he experienced a dramatic moment in which he was flooded by memories of being sexually abused by his older brother.

The persistent reexperience of the trauma is often the most dramatic and easily recognizable expression of PTSD. In this case, the reexperience occurred during intoxication and was then repressed, consistent with the blackout phenomenon found in both trauma and alcoholism. Incest or other trauma survivors who reexperience the trauma as intrusive memories, nightmares, flashbacks, *déjà vu,* or other similar experiences may or may not have conscious memory of the trauma. They may seek help more because of the disturbing nature of the recurring symptoms than because of the experience of the trauma itself. Survivors who experience periods of altered consciousness may behave as though they were again in the traumatic situation (flashbacks). This may involve a flood of emotion or regressed or violent behavior as they revert to the cognitive and behavioral coping strategies that they used as children during the traumatic experience (Figley 1985).

Reexperience phenomena may be spontaneous or may be precipitated by related stimuli. If the victim has no memory of the specific traumatic event, the precipitants may go unidentified. This can be especially confusing if the blackout or flashback involves idiosyncratic behavior, such as hiding in unusual places or crying out in garbled speech. Triggers that elicit reexperience phenomena are often concrete, idiosyncratic sensory stimuli similar to those present during the trauma, such as the smell of the perpetrator's cologne. Memories may also be triggered in therapy or in the process, with the patient revealing the incest to significant others while seeking their support (Figley 1985). Current nosology recognizes these recurrent experiences even when they occur during intoxicated states (APA 1987).

Avoidance and Numbing

A case example: L. was a thirty-year-old recovering alcoholic and grade school teacher who presented for treatment complaining that her life was passing her by. She had always wished for a happy marriage and children, a life stage that she had imagined would have been well under way by this age. Instead, she found that her friendships, including those she had made in AA, were superficial; she felt detached from her boyfriend and did not want to marry him. It was puzzling and frustrating to her that this should be so, since she had been working so hard on sobriety as a way to change her destiny. She recounted many horrible stories of her childhood in a large and chaotic family dominated by her father, a severely disturbed man who beat, sexually abused, and humiliated his wife and daughters.

✳   ✳   ✳

Currently accepted diagnostic criteria for PTSD emphasize avoidance and numbing as a critical part of the disorder (APA 1987). There may be psychogenic amnesia for aspects of the trauma. The survivor may recall most or all uncomfortable events of childhood related to the incest, such as rewards and punishments or even other instances of sexual abuse, but be unable to recall the specific incestuous acts. In many cases, energy may be mobilized to avoid two kinds of related stimuli: thoughts and feelings associated with the trauma, or activities that stimulate memories of the trauma. The amnesic survivor may be especially unaware of or puzzled by these avoidance attempts. This phenomenon may explain why M., the engaged banker, could not understand her discomfort with intimacy. There may also be decreased interest in important activities, such as hobbies. When recollections of the incest finally emerge, victims and their therapists report relief from confusion as pieces of the puzzle fall into place.

Use of alcohol or drugs can also provide a numbing experience, although this is not necessarily recognized as part of the official PTSD syndrome (Root 1989). Similar affective patterns are reported by adult children of alcoholics. Typical characteristics include feeling nonspecifically abnormal, having poor self-esteem, anhedonia, and difficulty with intimate relationships (Ackerman 1987). Perhaps these similar constellations are not coincidental.

Feeling detached or lacking ability for feelings is frequently ego dystonic, even when it is understood by victims as a consequence of childhood violation. There may be the sense that there is no desirable future, such as the belief that one will not or cannot have a productive career or a loving relationship. Victims may act this out by undermining satisfying work or relationships, or even through self-destructive activity (APA 1987). Substance abuse may help fulfill this prophecy.

Evidence is emerging that endorphins (opioid substances produced in the central nervous system) mediate reactions to stress that entail modulation of affect. They appear involved in perception of pain, stress, and depression and may also be involved in the sense of relief experienced by trauma victims who seek out further painful experiences such as self-mutilation or additional traumatic experiences (van der Kolk and Greenberg 1987; Schetky 1990). It is likely that central nervous system opioids produce psychological numbing in PTSD (van der Kolk et al 1989).

Persistent Increased Arousal

C. was a twenty-three-year-old graduate student in therapy for questionable anxiety and phobias that had been starting to interfere with her productivity. She often used alcohol and marijuana to cope in social situations, and was becoming concerned that she was starting to feel equally uncomfortable in the lab. She was afraid to use these substances at work, since lab work required fine motor coordination.

One day she reported that she had seen Hitchcock's film *Psycho* at the weekend film festival and had been unable to shake off uneasy feelings inspired by the shower murder scene. She had reverted to feeling uncomfortable in bathrooms, specifically in bathtubs, and felt especially uneasy as the water gurgled down the drain. Over the years, she had adjusted to this phobia by taking showers and never baths, but now she feared she might be unable to shower as well. Asked to concentrate more on the origin of her bathing problems, she recalled vague memories of having been moved temporarily to her aunt's home as a child, and that this had something to do with bathing. Later she called her aunt, who told her that before he died from his alcoholism, her father had been accused of making inappropriate sexual advances to her, including at night and when bathing and dressing her. Under court supervision, he had been treated for this, and she had been returned home. He continued to drink from time to time, however, and during these periods, her aunt reported, C. would become anxious and tended to regress to childlike behaviors. Although C. recalled these anxious periods, she had no memory of the sexual abuse.

It is generally accepted that the nervous system functions as part of the organism's defense system. The capacity to move instantaneously from a resting state to that of complete attention and readiness to act in self-defense is physiologically mediated by the sympathetic nervous system (Guyton 1986). This fight-or-flight response is perceived as a sudden, heightened state of arousal and may be accompanied by a pleasurable or uncomfortable sensation, sometimes referred to as a "rush." PTSD involves an ongoing, heightened state of readiness of the fight-or-flight response network, presumably derived from the need for self-defense during the original trauma (APA 1987).

A number of sympathetically mediated, physiologic phenomena

are associated with the ongoing state of hyperarousal (APA 1987), although they may not be recognized as being connected with other problems the victim is having. It is often the job of the clinician to link the symptoms to the underlying problem. Most dramatically, the survivor may have a brisk physiologic response when confronted with reminders of the trauma. Some examples include sweating, a sense of one's stomach sinking, or increased heart rate, similar to an anxiety or phobic disorder. Reminders that trigger the physiologic response may be concrete (taking a bath) or abstract (the sound of water gurgling down the drain.) Difficulty falling asleep or staying asleep may be a prominent concern; the latter may be associated with nightmares that are part of the reexperience phenomenon. Irritability may be associated with the need to feel in control, especially in threatening or intimate situations, and a limited capacity to express disagreement may precipitate angry outbursts. An exaggerated startle response can also precipitate angry outbursts, such as a great degree of surprise and distress when surprised from behind by a child shouting, "boo!"

Often, victims and their families are well acquainted with this problem and have made adjustments to it. Difficulties with concentration often go unrecognized by the victim as being part of the syndrome. Distractibility may be accompanied by hypervigilance, sometimes perceived as a sense of paranoia. These symptoms may be perceived as a personality change by significant others, who may then urge the victim to seek treatment.

In general, persistent arousal is not experienced at all times, but in response to significant stressors. This inability to modulate arousal may be especially striking in those who are otherwise emotionally constricted due to numbing of general responsiveness. An overall tendency to overreact to stress of any sort may occur, including extreme anxiety and/or inappropriate, sometimes aggressive activity, such as striking out at others. Presumably, the latter represents defensive actions that were learned at the time of the trauma. Overreactivity may also include social or emotional withdrawal to a degree uncalled for by the situation. Stressors evoking these responses may be external or internal, and depending on the victim's awareness of the existence of traumatization and PTSD, the connection between stressor and reaction may or may not be apparent (Krystal 1985). Essentially, the victim has lost the capacity to distinguish between minor problems and emergencies. Symptom patterns of aggression and withdrawal may be interpreted as part of a personality disorder, especially if the history of trauma has not been revealed (van der Kolk and Greenberg 1987).

Fitting the Pieces Together

A few aspects of the relationships among incest, substance abuse, and post-traumatic stress disorder have been presented. Family systems are stressed in situations of substance abuse and incest, which result in varying degrees of boundary violation and other dysfunction. PTSD and substance abuse both involve attempts to regulate memory and affect, and often occur together as incest sequelae. A number of theories attempt to explain how trauma leads to these and other pathological outcomes; the following sections review some of the theory and research that have potential to illuminate these relationships.

The causal relationship has been explored from a number of perspectives, including descriptive, dynamic, learning theories, and biologic mechanisms. As the evidence gets more complex, it becomes harder to remain affiliated with one school of thought. Some of the hypotheses being generated seem contrary, probably stemming from the fact that post-traumatic syndromes are diverse. How can substance abuse increase numbing in some survivors and increase arousal in others? There are more partial than complete answers, and clinicians working with traumatized substance abusers can only try to fit the pieces together as best they can. The next few decades promise to shed increased light on these interrelations. In the meantime, the continuing questions surrounding these problems promise to become increasingly interesting and clinically relevant.

The following sections briefly review some hypotheses that seem likely to become useful in clinical settings. First, some affective aspects are reviewed, including potential explanations for the disturbance of affective expression and how affect influences memory. This leads to the self-medication hypothesis, which has become increasingly popular. Some learning theory constructs follow, including learned helplessness, classical conditioning, and coping skills. Although these sections are brief, they refer to some perspectives that are often overlooked by dynamically and biologically trained therapists. They are worth considering, as they can be extremely helpful in single- and multiple-problem survivors and addicts. Some tentative but exciting theorizing about biological correlates of PTSD and addiction syndromes are reviewed. The reader is reminded that these are highly hypothetical; however, they can provide food for thought in our attempts to work with our patients to understand and overcome their problems.

Paucity of Affective Expression

Survivors and clinicians continually describe misleading presenting symptoms, such the vague dysphoria and other complaints noted above. A cognitive model (Fine 1990) explains this phenomenon as an overlearned response. Victims must integrate the reality of being violated with opposing evidence. An example of an opposing reality could be society's assumptions that the perpetrator is a protector and that the home is a safe place. Another could be direct denial when querying family members about whether the abuse occurred. In order to work within this inconsistent framework, victims learn not to trust the obvious. They become less able to integrate novel information, including being less able to perceive and adapt to nonabusive environments as being different from the home. This includes reinterpreting affective experience and can lead to presenting complaints that seem to have nothing to do with incest. Decreased capacity to integrate affective experience can explain dissociative phenomena, the ultimate inability to integrate opposing information.

An increasingly popular construct regarding the extreme inability to express emotions verbally is alexithymia. The lack of words to describe feelings may be accompanied by a paucity of internal affective experience. These difficulties with verbal expression of emotions may be fairly well circumscribed and not accompanied by verbal deficits in other domains. Thus, the alexithymic may be articulate in other areas and may not appear to be intellectually or otherwise impaired. Inability to discuss affect may be experienced by others as resistance to therapy or to other intimate relationships. Alexithymia may contribute to disturbed behavior that is meant to express internal distress, as in the case of J.'s brother, T., whose misbehaviors increased as his life fell apart.

Distrust of intimate relationships resulting from the betrayal of basic trust due to incest experiences may also be a factor in resistance, whether or not the incest is consciously remembered. This may explain why listlessness and dysphoria are common presenting complaints of incest survivors, as well as for addicts.

Affect and Memory

The connection between affect and memory (or between affective memory and cognitive memory) has led to a hypothesis that the former influences the latter. Affects are nonverbal, nonlogical processes that precede and accompany memory processing as well as other psychological functions, such as perceiving the world and one's place in it, and forming relationships. Massive sympathetic discharge in the brain preparing for fight or flight during traumatic experiences might help the formation of particularly enduring memories. Control of these pathways is diminished under conditions of stress and also during sleep, releasing increased numbers of affectively charged memories (van der Kolk and Greenberg 1987). This may be one explanation of why intrusive thoughts and nightmares occur under stressful conditions. In these situations, the body prepares for defense with a sympathetic discharge; this triggers the affectively affiliated memories of the trauma (Schetky 1990). It appears that the sympathetic discharge produces a non-specific effect: fight-flight readiness becomes confused with traumatic memories. This same mechanism might be responsible for the increase in symptoms in substance use and withdrawal, as described later in the sections on biologic effects and psychoendocrine theories.

For trauma survivors, affect flattening could be a defense against the fear of recalling and even reexperiencing the trauma, such as that employed by L. to survive with the memories of her family's extensive abuse at the hands of her father. In an attempt to avoid being overwhelmed by childhood memories, she became unable to experience depth or intimacy in her relationships. This constriction of intense or frightening feelings cannot be separated from that of other feelings, resulting in a generalized affective constriction (Krystal 1985).

Alcohol affects the brain's ability to coordinate attention to external events. It also affects the hippocampus, part of the brain's memory storage system (Bloom 1989). This may help explain why alcohol helps incest victims to tolerate their experience (and may have implications for the continued repression or loss of these memories) or to modulate emotional activity and its effects on recollection of traumatic experiences.

Substance Abuse and the Self-medication Hypothesis

One widely held model of substance abuse might be applied to explain why incest survivors initiate substance use. The self-medication hypothesis relates the use of substances to symptom relief—for example, the use of stimulants to counter depression (Khantzian 1990). In the case of traumatic experience, the substance may be used during the traumatic event to help the victim endure the circumstance, or may be employed later to alleviate PTSD symptoms. For example, the victim may drink "to forget" intrusive memories, or to overcome the distress of related events such as anxiety, shortness of breath, or a racing heart, upon returning to the family home (Root 1989). C.'s use of substances to overcome anxiety generated by repressed memories of bath-time incest may be one example. In some instances, substance use may be an effective remedy and may abate with psychiatric treatment (such as therapy with or without medication) or with the natural remission of the psychological symptoms (such as leaving the scene of the trauma.) In other cases, the addiction takes on a life of its own. In these cases, the victim-turned-addict believes the substance provides relief of symptoms, often despite objective evidence that symptoms are unchanged or worsened by substance use (Kosten and Krystal 1988).

Stimulation and Depletion of the Sympathetic Nervous System: Inescapable Shock and Learned Helplessness

One of the most striking features of PTSD is the contrast between states of arousal and numbing. One approach to this contrast supposes that overstimulation of the sympathetic nervous system results in eventual sympathetic depletion, with resultant decreases in arousal. Experimental animals have been exposed to distressing circumstances to study how they learn tasks that will free them from undesirable situations. Exposure to inescapable shock puts animals in a state of arousal that cannot be relieved by their efforts to escape. When animals are subjected to such inescapable stressors, they eventually appear to lose the capacity to learn. This response to inescapable shock is called *learned helplessness.*

Animals suffering learned helplessness have problems learning to escape from new stressors, even when escape is possible. They have decreased motivation for learning new strategies, and they exhibit chronic distress, presumably a correlate of demoralization (Kosten and Krystal 1988; van der Kolk and Greenberg 1987). In these cases, it appears that the sympathetic nervous system is activated to the point of exhaustion, leading to this alteration of easy arousal (or too much feeling) versus numbing (or too little feeling). The learned helplessness model may help explain why incest victims present complaints such as listlessness, alienation, and decreased level of function. It is also not unrelated to the hypothesis of alexithymia and other attempts to escape overwhelming affect (Krystal 1985). Cases like the dysphoric teenager J., or the disaffected schoolteacher L., may involve elements of learned helplessness.

Classical Conditioning

Classical conditioning can be used to explain the existence of persistent heightened arousal in PTSD. In traumatic situations, the actual danger is the unconditioned stimulus (US) that evokes acts of self-defense, the unconditioned response (UR). Other sensory stimuli are present, however, that are not threatening (the conditioned stimuli [CS]). Afterward, these neutral stimuli evoke the original response (now the conditioned response [CR]) to the trauma. This can be a very adaptive function. For example, in childhood abuse, recognition that the father is drunk again (CS, originally paired with abuse while the father was intoxicated) gets the child to leave the house (CR) before the father even sees the child.

Once learned, these associations may be applied even though the trauma is past and the subject is in a neutral or safe environment; this is the principle of *stimulus generalization* (Pavlov [1927] 1960). For C., the sound of water bubbling down a bathtub drain was the CS that elicited the CR of uneasiness. This model has been used to explain the state of persistent arousal (Kosten and Krystal 1988; van der Kolk and Greenberg 1987).

Behavioral Model: Coping Skills

Anticipation of relief from distress is potentiated when the addict has few or no other coping skills with which to face the conditioned stimuli. In this case, the addict imagines coping would be easier with a cigarette, a drink, or some other substance. A desire for the substance's effect to relieve the internal distress experienced in the stressful situation enhances the conditioned response. The addict who began using drugs to get through the incest situation and who has not developed other coping mechanisms may crave those same drugs in other stressful situations. The existence or severity of physical dependence on the substance seems to affect this cognitive process significantly (Marlatt 1985). For example, N.'s mother may have started using alcohol and drugs to tolerate the incest and quell the associated memories. As her addiction progressed, she probably turned to substances to cope with the stresses of daily life as a single parent.

Classical Conditioning and Biological Effects of Alcohol and Drug Withdrawal on PTSD

Sedative substances, such as alcohol, benzodiazepines, barbiturates, and opiates, are known to suppress sympathetic response and PTSD symptoms acutely. It is believed that this quality is the basis for the initiation of substance abuse in some trauma victims. Chronic substance use leads to tolerance for these effects, however, sometimes to the point where the substances have no anxiolytic effect at all.

Just as the use of alcohol and drugs appears to stimulate similar neurobiologic pathways to those of PTSD, withdrawal from alcohol and drugs also seems to affect these systems. Here, the sympathetic nervous system is of special interest. Symptom suppression and exacerbation seem at least partially mediated by the central sympathetic nervous system. Alcohol, sedative drugs (such as benzodiazepines), or opioids initially alleviate anxiety, flashbacks, or hyperarousal symptoms. Withdrawal from these substances is likely to have the opposite effect, however, mediated at least in part by the sympathetic nervous system (Kosten and Krystal, 1988). In withdrawal states, the irritable sympathetic nervous system increases activity, thus exacerbating both withdrawal and PTSD symptoms. A person like P., drinking heavily with his fraternity brothers in social situations, would be a likely candidate for such problems. It has been suggested that the coexistence of addiction and PTSD exacerbates alcohol and drug withdrawal due to additive effects. A somewhat more controversial hypothesis along these lines is that flashbacks during withdrawal are actually polysensory hallucinations caused by withdrawal alone (Kosten and Krystal 1988).

Drug and alcohol cravings can be understood as conditioned responses (CR) that occur when addicts are confronted with either concrete or abstract reminders (CS) of their drug abuse (UCR). Craving appears to involve sympathetic/adrenergic as well as other neurotransmitter activity in the brain (Wise 1988). Addicts with PTSD often confuse their PTSD symptoms with craving and with arousal in general, because the involvement of sympathetic pathways produces similar physical sensation in both craving and arousal. Thus, similar bodily sensations in craving and arousal may promote a cognitive tendency to associate them emotionally. This may be particularly problematic for those who have a baseline difficulty distinguishing affective states (Kosten and Krystal 1988; Krystal 1978). If flashbacks of the traumatic experience occur only during intoxication or withdrawal, identification of childhood trauma can be difficult. Dysphoria or emotional distress of any sort may lead to hyperarousal states that may then be confused with alcohol or drug withdrawal, leading the individual to turn to substance use, which is likely to exacerbate the whole problem (Kosten and Krystal (1988).

Psychoendocrine Theories

A number of explanations of the symptoms of both substance abuse and PTSD appear to involve the sympathetic nervous system and its neurotransmitters, epinephrine and norepinephrine, including some signs and symptoms of alcohol withdrawal and of persistent hyperarousal in PTSD. This may be the basis of increased PTSD symptoms during alcohol and possibly other drug use. Intoxication may provide a memory-dampening mechanism that is adrenergically mediated (Bloom 1989). The various learning hypotheses indicate that sympathetically mediated suppression of distress may be important in the reinforcing effects of substance abuse. Endogenous opioid systems, including endorphins, appear active in both the maintenance of pleasurable and emotionally blunted states, possibly connecting opiate use of withdrawal to ongoing PTSD experiences. Substance abuse may be initiated to help tolerate affective distress of traumatization.

The hormonal aspects of substance abuse and PTSD are not yet fully elucidated. In addition to the likelihood that the sympathetic and endogenous opioid systems are important in the development and maintenance of symptoms, corticosteroids (cortisol and the like) that mediate the body's response to stress, sex hormones (such as testosterone) that are involved in modulating aggression, and thyroid hormones that are involved in regulating energy levels may also be involved (Mason et al. 1990). The final psychoendocrine model of PTSD is certain to be intricate and complex.

Summary

Substance abuse and post-traumatic stress disorder appear to be common sequelae of incest. The current practice of subspecializations in treating incest, substance abuse, and PTSD has led to advances in each field. It now seems clear, however, that it is time for workers in these fields to share their clinical expertise to develop more comprehensive diagnostic and treatment approaches to these complicated problems.

First, diagnostic thinking needs to be expanded. Clinicians need to increase their suspicion of incest whether or not such a history is revealed or remembered, especially when substance abuse is present. Looking for symptoms of PTSD can be helpful here. Symptoms that do not seem to fit together may then fall easily into place.

Family systems approaches can provide clarity whether the patient presents with the family or alone, in which case the clinician may examine the family by history. Recognizing signs of role reassignment, over- and undercompensation, difficulty establishing intimate relationships, and regression in family members should alert the clinician to suspect incest and to beware family denials and secrets.

Diagnosing PTSD from a disparate jumble of vague complaints can open the door to suspected childhood traumatization and can help the clinician seek further evidence. Understanding some of the dynamic forces that are at work regulating memory and affect can help the clinician select a helpful pace in therapy. Learning theory may provide a base for understanding attitudes and repetitive choices and behaviors. Evidence of sympathetic involvement in the maintenance of PTSD symptoms may provide a basis for behavioral and pharmacologic management of incest victims. Not surprisingly, other nervous system components (such as serotonergic, dopaminergic, and endogenous opioids) appear to be involved as well. The theories and evidence presented in this chapter outline a fraction of the complex picture that is developing to explain the multiply determined sequelae of trauma.

If there is any simple message here, it is for clinicians to raise the level of suspicion of trauma when confronted with patients, particularly women, who abuse substances. Similarly, ill-defined complaints of dysphoria, alienation, nightmares, or panic attacks should alert the clinician to watch for evidence of traumatic experiences that may be repressed or withheld.

Combining exploratory work with supportive and cognitive-behavioral techniques and pharmacologic management as indicated may prove to be most helpful as our patients seek the causes of their symptoms. Knowledge of the treatment strategies for substance abuse will often be necessary to help patients approach their own history and create workable relationships with the important people in their lives.

References

Ackerman, R. J. (1987). *Let Go and Grow: Recovery for Adult Children of Alcoholics.* Pompano Beach, FL: Health Communications.

American Psychiatric Association (1987). *Diagnostic and Statistical Manual of Mental Disorders* (3rd Ed., Rev.). Washington, D.C.: American Psychiatric Press.

Barnes, G. M. (1990). Impact of the family on adolescent drinking problems. In R. L. Collins, K. E. Leonard, & J. S. Searles, (Eds.), *Alcohol and the Family: Research and Clinical Perspectives.* New York: Guilford.

Benedek, E. P. (1984). The silent scream: countertransference reactions to victims. *American Journal of Social Psychiatry IV,* 3:49–52.

Bennett, L. A., and Wolin, S. J. (1990). Family culture and alcoholism transmission. In R. L. Collins, K. E. Leonard, & J. S. Searles (Eds.), *Alcohol and the Family: Research and Clinical Perspectives.* New York: Guilford.

Bepko, C., and Krestan, J. A. (1985). *The Responsibility Trap: A Blueprint for Treating the Alcoholic Family.* New York: Free Press.

Bloom, F. E. (1989). Neurobiology of alcohol action and alcoholism. In A. Tasman, R. E. Hales, and A. J. Francis (Eds.), *American Psychiatric Press Review of Psychiatry, Vol. 8.* Washington, DC: American Psychiatric Press.

Blume, S. B. (1986). Women and alcohol: A review. *Journal of the American Medical Association* 256:1467–70.

Briere, J., and Runtz, M. (1988). Post sexual abuse trauma. In G. E. Wyatt & G. J. Powell (Eds.), *Lasting Effects of Child Sexual Abuse.* London: Sage.

Browne, A., and Finklehor, D. (1986). Impact of child sexual abuse: A review of the literature. *Psychological Bulletin* 99:66–67.

Calof, D. (1988). Treating adult survivors of incest and child abuse (workshop presented at the Family Health Network Symposium, Washington, DC). In C. A. Courtois, *Healing the Incest Wound: Adult Survivors in Therapy.* New York: W. W. Norton.

Courtois, C. A. (1988). *Healing the Incest Wound: Adult Survivors in Therapy.* New York: W. W. Norton.

Deutsche, C. (1982). *Broken Bottles, Broken Dreams: Understanding and Helping the Children of Alcoholics.* New York: Teachers College Press.

Donaldson, M. A., and Gardner, R., Jr. (1985). Diagnosis and treatment of traumatic stress among women after childhood incest. In C. R. Figley (Ed.), *Trauma and Its Wake: The Study and Treatment of Post-Traumatic Stress Disorder.* New York: Brunner/Mazel.

Figley, C. R. (1985). From victim to survivor: Social responsibility in the wake of catastrophe. In C. R. Figley (Ed.), *Trauma and Its Wake: The Study and Treatment of Post-Traumatic Stress Disorder.* New York: Brunner/Mazel.

Fine, C. G. (1990). The cognitive sequelae of incest. In R. P. Kluft (Ed.), *Incest-Related Syndromes of Adult Psycopathology.* Washington, D.C.: American Psychiatric Press.

Freud, S. (1955). Introductory lectures of psychoanalysis. In J. Strachey (Ed. & Trans.), *The Standard Edition of the Complete Psychological Works of Sigmund Freud.* London: Hogarth Press. (Original work published in 1933).

Gelinas, D. J. (1983). The persisting negative effects of Incest. *Psychiatry* 46:312–32.

Goodwin, J. (1985). Post-traumatic symptoms in incest victims. In S. Eth & R. S. Pynoos (Eds.), *Post-Traumatic Stress Disorder in Children.* Washington, D.C.: American Psychiatric Press.

Guyton, A. C. (1986). *Textbook of Medical Physiology* (7th Ed.). Philadelphia: W. B. Saunders.

Herman, J., & Hirschman, L. (1981). Families at risk for father-daughter incest. *American Journal of Psychiatry* 138:967–70.

Khantzian, E. J. (1990). Self-regulation and self-medication factors in alcoholism and addictions: Similarities and differences. In M. Galanter (Ed.), *Recent Developments in Alcoholism, Vol. 8.* New York: Plenum.

Kosten, T. R., & Krystal, J. (1988). Biological mechanisms in posttraumatic stress disorder: Relevance for substance abuse. In M. Galanter (Ed.), *Recent Developments in Alcoholism, Vol. 6.* New York: Plenum.

Krystal, H. (1985). Trauma and the stimulus barrier. *Psychoanalytic Inquiry* 5:131–61.

Leonard, K. E. (1990). Marital functioning among episodic and steady alcoholics. In R. L. Collins, K. E. Leonard, & J. S. Searles, (Eds.), *Alcohol and the Family: Research and Clinical Perspectives.* New York: Guilford.

Lindberg, F. H., & Distad, L. J. (1985). Post-traumatic stress disorders in women who experienced childhood incest. *Child Abuse and Neglect* 9:329–34.

Marlatt, G. A. (1985). Cognitive factors in the relapse process. In G. A.

Marlatt & J. R. Gordon (Eds.), *Relapse Prevention: Maintenance Strategies in the Treatment of Addictive Behaviors*. New York: Guilford.

Mason, J. W., Giller, E. L., Kosten, T. R., & Yehuda, R. (1990). Psychoendocrine approaches to the diagnosis and pathogenesis of posttraumatic stress disorder. In E. L. Giller, Jr. (Ed.), *Biological Assessment and Treatment of Posttraumatic Stress Disorder*. Washington, D.C.: American Psychiatric Press.

Meiselman, K. C. (1981). *Incest: A Psychological Study of Causes and Effects with Treatment Recommendations*. San Francisco: Jossey-Bass.

Nace, E. P. (1988). Posttraumatic stress disorder and substance abuse: Clinical issues. In M. Galanter (Ed.), *Recent Developments in Alcoholism*, Vol. 6. New York: Plenum.

O'Farrell, T. (1990). Sexual functioning of male alcoholics. In R. L. Collins, K. E. Leonard, & J. S. Searles (Eds.), *Alcohol and the Family: Research and Clinical Perspectives*. New York: Guilford.

Ogden, T. H. (1979). "On Projective Identification." *International Journal of Psychoanalysis* 60:357–73.

Pavlov, I. P. (1960). *Conditioned Reflexes: An Investigation of the Physiological Activity of the Cerebral Cortex* (G. V. Anrep, Ed. & Trans.). New York: Dover. (Original work published in 1927)

Root, M. P. P. (1989). Treatment failures: The role of sexual victimization in women's addictive behavior. *American Journal of Orthopsychiatry* 59:542–49.

Russell, D. E. H. (1986). *The Secret Trauma: Incest in the Lives of Girls and Women*. New York: Basic Books.

Schetky, D. H. (1990). A review of the literature on the long-term effects of child sexual abuse. In R. P. Kluft (Ed.), *Incest-Related Syndromes of Adult Psycopathology*. Washington, DC: American Psychiatric Press.

Skinner, B. F. (1953). *Science and Human Behavior*. New York: Macmillan.

Steinglass, P. (1982). The roles of alcohol in family systems. In J. Orford & J. Harwin (Eds.), *Alcohol and the Family*. London: Croom Helm.

Trimble, M. R. (1985). Post-traumatic stress disorder: History of a concept. In C. R. Figley (Ed.), *Trauma and Its Wake: The Study and Treatment of Post-Traumatic Stress Disorder*. New York: Brunner/Mazel.

van der Kolk, B. A., & Greenberg, M. S. (1987). The psychobiology of the trauma response: Hyperarousal, constriction, and addiction to traumatic reexposure. In B. A. van der Kolk (Ed.), *Psychological Trauma*. Washington, DC: American Psychiatric Press.

van der Kolk, B. A., Greenberg, M. S., Orr, S. P., & Pitman R. K. (1989). Endogenous opioids, stress induced analgesia, and posttraumatic stress disorder. *Psychopharmacology Bulletin* 25:417–21.

Wegscheider, S. (1981). *Another Chance: Hope and Health for the Alcoholic Family*. Palo Alto, CA: Science and Behavior Books.

Weinstein, S. K. (1955). *Incest Behavior*. New York: Citadel.

Wilson, J. P., Smith, W. K., & Johnson, S. K. (1985). A comparative analysis of PTSD among various survivor groups. In C. R. Figley (Ed.), *Trauma and Its Wake: The Study and Treatment of Post-Traumatic Stress Disorder.* New York: Brunner/Mazel.

Wise, R. A. (1988). The neurobiology of craving: Implications for the understanding and treatment of addiction. *Journal of Abnormal Psychology* 97:118–32.

7

Long Night's Journey into Day: The Treatment of Sexual Abuse among Substance-abusing Women

Kathleen Bollerud

> None of us can help the things that life has done to us. They're done before you realize it, and once they're done they make you do other things until at last everything comes between you and what you'd like to be, and you've lost your true self forever.
> —Eugene O'Neill

O'Neill's (1956) lament in the play *Long Day's Journey Into Night* is particularly poignant for women who have been sexually abused in childhood and subsequently have become chemically dependent. The tragedy is that by virtue of being abused as children, these women may be both physiologically and psychologically vulnerable to addiction (van der Kolk and Herman 1987). This association between victimization and substance abuse is noted in both research and clinical reports (Coleman 1987; Evans and Schaefer 1987; Herman 1981; Schaefer and Evans 1987).

Researchers posit that trauma victims may experience chronic hyperarousal, an alteration of the central nervous system that contributes to heightened vulnerability to addiction. Van der Kolk (1989) suggests that trauma victims may experience alterations in the levels of several neurotransmitters, including norepinephrine and serotonin, as well as dysregulation of the endogenous opioid system. These changes can lead to reduced or ineffective coping and self-soothing strategies. As a result, trauma victims may attempt to neutralize their hyperarousal with a variety of addictive behaviors.

In addition to physiological changes, a number of psychological symptoms can make trauma victims vulnerable to substance abuse. Women who experience symptoms of post-traumatic stress disorder (PTSD) show such serious problems as persistent fear, anxiety, depression, and anger, they also frequently experience dissociative symptoms presenting as alterations in memory, consciousness, and identity. Alcohol and drugs are often used to alter mood, decrease intrusive recall, decrease affective lability, or increase affective expression.

Terr (1990) describes a loss of belief in the future among victims of childhood trauma. She reports that victimized children do not believe that they will live a normal life span or have significant relationships and careers. In a similar manner, many substance abusers report the belief that they will die in young adulthood. Although this expectation of early death may be realistic, given the drug abuser's life-style, this self-fulfilling prophecy also may be a manifestation of the futurelessness described by abused children. Furthermore, the traumatized child's loss of future orientation may increase vulnerability to the immediate gratification of substance use.

Few women make a conscious connection between their victimization and substance abuse (Russell 1986). Yandow (1989), however, estimates that as many as 75% of women in treatment settings for alcoholism have a history of sexual abuse that generally started in childhood and frequently continued until the initiation of treatment. Alcoholic women with post-traumatic symptoms report more anxiety and depression in early sobriety and may be more vulnerable to relapse (Kovach 1986).

This chapter suggests a model to guide the outpatient treatment of sexually abused, chemically dependent women who diagnostically fit within the range of post-traumatic or dissociative disorders. Though much of this material may be useful in the treatment of men, this chapter focuses on women because some of the clinical manifestations of trauma-related syndromes appear to be gender related. For example, male victims of sexual abuse frequently have concerns about homosexuality, whereas female victims are more likely to have concerns about male domination. Also, research indicates that abused males tend to identify with the aggressor and later victimize others, whereas abused women are prone to become attached to abusive men and to allow themselves and their children to be victimized further (van der Kolk 1989).

The model described in this chapter is a multimodal approach to recovery that incorporates twelve-step programs, individual psychotherapy, and short-term specialized group treatment. The individual-psychotherapy component is based on a phase model for the treatment of trauma described by Brown and Fromm (1986), as well as therapeutic strategies for the treatment of sexual abuse elaborated by Courtois (1988), Gelinas (1989), and Herman (1981). The model for specialized group psychotherapy is based on the work of Herman and Schatzow (1984).

Patient Assessment

The inherent danger in assessing patients with comorbidity for substance abuse and trauma-related disorders is that a diagnosis will be made prematurely, without adequate attention to the secondary diagnosis. Mental health and substance abuse professionals often lack training in their complementary disciplines and, therefore, may inadvertently disregard the assessment of dissociative disorders among chemically dependent patients or substance abuse among trauma victims. Even the most forthcoming patient with a background of victimization and substance abuse is seldom aware of the range of her symptoms and has little basis to judge what is "normal" or what should be reported to her therapist. In addition, these patients, enmeshed in a conspiracy of silence, are frequently adept at evasiveness and misinformation. The stigma associated with both sexual victimization and substance abuse leads to extremes of secrecy and lying.

The symptoms associated with PTSD (American Psychiatric Association [APA] 1987) involve reexperiencing the traumatic event, avoiding stimuli associated with the event, and increased arousal. The trauma may be reexperienced in a variety of ways, including nightmares, daydreams, flashbacks, and reliving the event without awareness of the initial trauma through repetition compulsion. Alcohol and drugs frequently play a role in compulsive reenactment and revictimization of trauma victims. Avoidant behaviors may include deliberate efforts to escape thoughts and feelings associated with the event, constriction of affect, and emotional numbing. Mood-altering substances are frequently used to achieve this relief from painful affects. Persistent symptoms of arousal include difficulty falling or staying asleep, hypervigilance, and exaggerated startle response. Patients may also experience difficulty in modulating aggressive affects.

In dissociative disorders, the predominant features are disturbances or alterations in the normally integrative functions of identity, memory, and consciousness. The hallmark symptoms associated with DD (APA 1987) include "loss of time" (amnesias or inability to recall important events or personal information), depersonalization (the experience of feeling detached from or outside of one's body), and derealization (feeling like an automaton or as if in a dream). The more severe and/or ritualistic the abuse suffered as a child, the more fragmented the adult personality is likely to be. This type of abuse, especially when it occurs with parents or family members, is frequently associated with multiple personality disorder (MPD; Braun 1990).

Once a history of substance abuse or childhood sexual abuse has been obtained, the clinician should routinely interview for symptoms of PTSD or DD. Dissociative disorders often present with vague and ambiguous symptoms that can be falsely attributed to substance abuse. For example, dissociating substance abusers often assume amnesias are "blackouts". This loss of time may arouse little concern in a patient who lacks curiosity due to both residual effects of substance abuse and the *la belle indifference* characteristic of dissociative defenses. Alternately, a patient who is aware of this extensive forgetting may be embarrassed to describe her distress and mask or confabulate to disguise it.

It is good practice to administer the Dissociative Events Scale (DES; Ross, Norton, and Anderson 1988) routinely to any patient whose symptom picture suggests PTSD or DD with or without a reported history of childhood sexual abuse. In a clinical (as opposed to research) setting, the scale can be presented in an interview format, and upon completion, the therapist can ask the patient to elaborate on any endorsed items. This procedure is particularly helpful in identifying amnesias, depersonalization, and derealization, as well as symptoms suggestive of MPD. The patient should also be questioned in detail about Schneiderian first-rank symptoms, especially auditory hallucinations (voices in one's head) and passive-influence phenomena (the feeling that someone is trying to influence or control one's mind).

Stages of Treatment

A major challenge to the therapist in dealing with the dually diagnosed patient is to know which symptoms should be treated in which order. Brown and Fromm (1986, p. 277) have elaborated a phase model for the treatment of trauma that provides guidance in dealing with the complex issues presented by these patients. The following is an adaptation of this model that is focused on the needs of the dually diagnosed chemically dependent trauma survivor. Though the stages themselves appear discrete, progress in treatment often follows a more circuitous and overlapping route. The phases of treatment are:

1. Stabilization
2. Memory and affect integration
3. Self and self-esteem development

Stabilization

Frequently, chemically dependent trauma victims will present for treatment with life-threatening symptoms, such as substance abuse and suicidal or homicidal behaviors. The goal of the stabilization phase is to ensure the patient's safety while she acquires the knowledge and coping skills necessary to proceed with therapy. As a general rule, on an outpatient basis, the chemically dependent person must achieve a stable sobriety before she is capable of dealing with traumatic material. Some more flexibility may be indicated for the patient with MPD, as it may not be possible for her to maintain sobriety across the entire personality system early in treatment.

This need for sobriety is frequently met with great resistance by the patient and hesitation on the part of the therapist. Both patient and therapist can underestimate the effect of substance abuse on emotional and cognitive functioning; the affective lability associated with chemical dependency can be confused with a cathartic response to traumatic material.

Without a stable sobriety, the patient often experiences intense cravings for mood-altering substances either before or after dealing with traumatic memories. She may also attempt to explore traumatic memories before she is able to sustain the psychological assaults inherent in remembering and feeling the abuse. Thus, she can easily be overwhelmed and experience recurrent life-threatening relapses. To protect the patient from the perceived failure of relapse, adequate time must be spent achieving a foundation of sobriety. Early clinical decisions need to focus on assessing the level of support she will need in order to do this. A model for the treatment of trauma-related syndromes among chemically dependent inpatients has been articulated by Bollerud (1990). For outpatients, Alcoholics Anonymous (AA) and other twelve-step programs are the primary treatment modality in early sobriety. AA provides a program of recovery that gives concrete supports and teaches strategies for managing daily stress. Individual psychotherapy should be seen as an adjunct to this twelve-step work.

In the individual psychotherapy, development of a therapeutic alliance can be problematic, because the patient has suffered abuses of power and betrayal by loved ones. The extent of her fear and mistrust is rarely evident, as it is masked by a submissive or angry demeanor; however, she is often acutely sensitive to issues of power. The patient should be helped to understand that difficulties with trust are related to the initial abuse and that she can experience vulnerability without being attacked or exploited.

Early in treatment, the patient should be advised that she may be coping with coexisting disorders (addiction and post-traumatic distress), each of which require specialized treatment in order to achieve long-term recovery. Education about the nature of addiction and the process of recovery from sexual violence is helpful. Symptoms and defenses should be understood as reactions to abuse (Courtois 1988). This approach demystifies the treatment process and, to some extent, equalizes the therapy relationship as it helps the patient to understand how her current difficulties may have developed. This cognitive framework is also a powerful resource in managing symptoms, as it decreases the patient's fearfulness and shame.

In addition to education and twelve-step work, the therapist can provide a variety of concrete problem-solving tools to help the patient cope with intrusive post-traumatic symptoms such as flashbacks. A number of anxiety management techniques, such as deep breathing, relaxation training, and exercise, can be introduced (Brown and Fromm 1986). In situations where the patient is incapacitated by anxiety or depression, referral for medication may be appropriate; it must be kept in mind, however, that minor tranquilizers are contraindicated for substance abusers. Any acting out in the form of life-threatening behaviors or relapse indicates that the patient is not ready to proceed with the uncovering work.

Clinical Example. Sandra was a twenty-nine-year-old woman first seen for treatment in a drug and alcohol rehabilitation facility. In addition to alcoholism, Sandra manifested many symptoms suggestive of PTSD. During her hospitalization, she disclosed a history of multiple rapes during her adolescence.

Following hospitalization, Sandra was referred to AA and individual psychotherapy. Sobriety was defined as a foundation for the outpatient work. Although Sandra was motivated for treatment of the sexual abuse, she minimized the effects of alcohol on her life. She attended AA only sporadically and would not participate in the meetings or get a sponsor. She would frequently drink while driving home from therapy sessions and, finally, attended a session after having several drinks. During her drinking, Sandra was quite dangerous to herself and others.

It became clear that treatment for the sexual abuse was not beneficial to her at that time. Therefore, outpatient psychotherapy was suspended until sobriety could be firmly established. This decision (which was very painful for Sandra and her therapist), as well as several episodes of suicidal behavior while intoxicated, gradually penetrated the denial surrounding her alcoholism. Sandra eventually became active in AA and obtained a sponsor. During this time, she and the therapist communicated through periodic letters. Sandra and the therapist agreed to reengage in outpatient psychotherapy after one year of sobriety.

Integration

The goals of the integration phase are to help the patient develop adaptive techniques for coping with the feelings associated with the abuse. During this stage, treatment is actively directed toward the trauma. For some patients whose memory of the actual trauma is repressed or dissociated, the therapeutic task is memory enhancement or to provide a cognitive frame for the experienced floods of feeling. For others who remember the trauma but have little or no access to the feelings associated with it, the therapeutic task is affect enhancement. For most patients, integration involves a combination of both affect and memory enhancement. Working through the trauma requires bringing the memories and feelings together. Brown and Fromm (1986) refer to this process as "uncovering" and describe a progression in which the patient is exposed to varying "doses" of disavowed affects and memories as she is able to integrate them into conscious experience. Hypnotic and art therapy techniques are particularly helpful in this process. These techniques appear to bypass the rigid defensive structure that has isolated the patient's memories and feelings over the years.

In preparation for memory enhancement, Brown and Fromm (1986) teach the patient to use hypnosis to explore protective and soothing imagery. This technique builds on the relaxation training used in the stabilization phase. In trance, the patient is instructed to imagine a place where she feels especially safe and protected. Over time, she is encouraged to explore a series of these scenes, which will eventually serve as the base of operations for further exploratory and uncovering work. When the patient is able to locate and maintain a safe place easily, she is ready to begin uncovering. Her "safe place" will serve as a refuge should the traumatic material become overwhelming.

As the uncovering progresses, the therapist can help the patient to develop adaptive defenses to deal with intrusive symptoms. Anxiety management techniques can also be helpful in this regard. For example, a patient who is flooded with a frightening emotion can be asked to "hold" the feeling for a brief interval (for example, five to ten seconds). Paradoxically, holding a feeling (rather than attempting to escape it) allows the emotion to pass and dissipate. Alternately, using hypnoprojective techniques such as imagining a television set, the patient can view frightening situations at a distance (Brown and Fromm 1986). In this way, the amount of affect experienced while recalling the traumatic event is regulated. The purpose of these techniques is to help the patient separate the observing from the experiencing ego: the observing ego retains control while the experiencing ego relives certain aspects of the traumatic situation (Brown and Fromm 1986). Gradually the flashbacks and memory fragments lose their terrifying intensity and become tolerable, albeit painful, opportunities for learning what happened.

Watkins (1971) describes a hypnotic technique to regain forgotten events called the "affect bridge." In trance, the patient can be moved experientially from a present emotion to the past incident over affect common to the two events. This technique is particularly helpful for patients who are experiencing storms of emotion that have no conscious precipitant.

Clinical Example. Elizabeth is a thirty-four-year-old woman who had somatic sensations that appeared related to childhood sexual abuse without any conscious memories to explain the phenomenon. She experienced intense fear in anticipation of a therapy session in which uncovering work was planned. This fear was intensified through the affect-bridge technique, and she was age regressed to an earlier time when she had experienced terror. In the trance state, Elizabeth was able to recall a horrifying rape by her uncle that occurred when she was six-years old. She recounted the following episode:

> Oh, fire, I see fire. There is a grate in the floor which is over the furnace. I can look down and see the furnace. Uncle Bob is saying to me, "I can put you in there, I can burn you. Come sit on my lap; it's much nicer than being down in that fire." I want to go and sit on his lap if he will hold me and be nice, but I know he will try doing those things to me and I don't want that. But then he tells me about the fire some more and I am afraid, so I go and sit in his lap. He is touching me down there. He is trying to put his fingers into me. No it's not his fingers, it's that snake! He is pushing it into me. It's too big for me; it's tearing me apart! It's going to kill me!

In a trance state, Elizabeth was able to access the source of the anxiety and physical pain that had haunted her adult life. She was finally able to connect those feelings to actual events. This knowledge brought significant relief as it enabled Elizabeth to view herself with more compassion.

Art therapy techniques can also be helpful for memory or affect enhancement. Mayer (1983) describes a number of these techniques. Patients can be asked to draw fragments of dreams or memories; the intense concentration inherent in the drawing process often elicits material that might otherwise be inaccessible. In the draw-the-event series, the patient draws herself before, during, and after the abuse. These images can be quite powerful, as they highlight and clarify the patient's experience of changes in her identity and self-representation as a result of the abuse.

Clinical Example. At thirteen years of age, a young gymnast, Maria, accompanied several neighborhood boys to the home of a friend. While there, she was given alcohol for the first time. She became extremely intoxicated and recalls passing out as she was raped by her "friends." Her next memory is of returning home with her clothes in shreds. Maria's family blamed her for precipitating the attack. Shortly after the rape, they moved from the area, effectively ending her athletic career. She began drinking and using drugs with increasing frequency. She became pregnant at sixteen years old and married. Her husband was an alcoholic who abused her. Five years later, Maria had two children and was divorced.

In her mid-thirties, Maria got sober with the help of AA. After several years, however, she was depressed and prone to rages. Although she had stabilized her self-destructive behavior in AA, Maria had not worked through the profound impact of the rape on her life. In an effort to help her gain access to the emotions associated with the rape, she was asked to draw herself before, during, and after the event. As she drew, Maria commented:

> [Before:] I was a normal little girl. Just your typical, average, happy-go-lucky, nothing-special-about-you kid. These were my friends, we grew up together. [During:] And then they raped me. I became hollow, empty, a silent shell. No mouth, just staring eyes. [After:] Afterwards, I tried to pretend I was the same girl, but now it's as if I have two sets of eyes looking at the world, and I'm filled with emptiness.

This exercise helped Maria to connect her floods of sadness and rage with her experience as a victim. She was able to see these emotions as sequelae to a pivotal trauma in her development, rather than as evidence for her "badness." These drawings produced a powerful metaphor for Maria's ongoing treatment as she struggled to regain a voice for her "hollow, empty shell."

Self and Self-Esteem Development

The experience of dehumanizing violence affects identity development and self-esteem, because it challenges the most basic assumptions about the self as intrinsically worthy (Reiker 1986). As a result, there tend to be characteristic distortions in the sense of self as experienced by victims of trauma. These distortions in identity center around ego functions disrupted by the sexual violence: the management of aggression, interpersonal efficacy, and sexuality.

As van der Kolk (1989) notes, anger directed against the self or others is always a central problem in the lives of people who have been violated. Typically this anger, a manifestation of identification with the aggressor, manifests itself as an experience of the self as enraged or dangerous. Brown and Fromm (1986) describe this negative introject as the "killer self." This fragment of the self can lead to impulsive, aggressive acting out as the patient is unable to control her rage. Alternately, she is frightened by these aggressive urges and consequently inhibits normal aggression, which leaves her vulnerable to revictimization.

Clinical Example. Martha was a forty-year-old victim of incest by her father and sadistic abuse by her mother. After many years of alcoholism and prostitution, she was able to regain sobriety in her mid-thirties. She entered outpatient psychotherapy because of unremitting depression and an inability to develop a satisfying life-style. Her presentation was of a depleted person who had been living marginally, unable to pursue a career or relationships. After twelve months in treatment focusing on her abuse, Martha reported a series of dreams that vividly portrayed some resolution of her negative introjects. The elaboration of this material enabled her to work through her profound self-devaluation. These dreams provide a clue to her emerging celebration of herself as a survivor. The following dream is a manifestation of the "killer self":

> I dreamed I was in a beautiful forest waiting for my lover. All around me were gorgeous trees and beautiful undergrowth. I knew that my lover was coming, but I didn't know who he was. I was very excited and stimulated. I could hear his footsteps coming through the forest, and I became more and more euphoric. As he approached and I saw his shadow coming, I looked down to a pool of water at my own face. I saw that I was a wolf with big fangs and that the excitement that I was feeling was not passion but blood lust. I was excited because he was my father, and I was going to kill him.

A second negative introject, the "victim self," develops from the experience of the self-as-object. As a result of horrifying helplessness, the victim of abuse often develops an inappropriate passivity in interpersonal relationships that can lead to revictimization. She is caught in a negative spiral in which she feels increasingly vulnerable and deserving of abuse (van der Kolk 1989). Martha related the following dream, which illustrates her symbolic resolution of this self-devaluation:

> I dreamed that I was in my family, only I did not have my own body. Rather, I was part of my family but watching. I saw my family beating up on a little girl. They were kicking her, calling her names, and abusing her. Eventually, they threw her out and dumped her in the gutter. I saw my father come and pick up the little girl, and I said to him, "You pervert. That's just like you." I was part of abusing the little girl. I called her names and kicked her. I thought she deserved everything that she got. But finally in my dream, I realized that it wasn't the little girl's fault, that she really wasn't doing anything except lying there and taking it all. So I decided to save her, and I hid her under the couch and I waited till nobody was looking. Then I picked her up and carried her out of the house.

It was strange to see that I was the little girl and that I could save her.

A third negative introject seen among victims of sexual violence is the experience of the self as sexually devalued. Childhood sexual overstimulation can lead to premature erotization and sexualization of relationships. Victims often become promiscuous and are at high risk of becoming prostitutes (James and Meyerding 1977). Confusing cause and effect, sexual abuse victims frequently believe that these behaviors are shameful aspects of themselves that contributed to their selection as victims. Chemically dependent women are particularly vulnerable to this devaluation because of ego-dystonic sexual activities that they may have engaged in while intoxicated.

In treatment, the therapist must be quite active in countering negative self-perceptions and self-depreciation. It is important to draw attention to these unrealistic self-representations. An alert therapist highlights these introjects each time they are verbalized; this strategy can bring conscious attention to an unconscious "truth" about the self that the patient has accepted. Interpersonal events are reframed so that the patient can understand that she has suffered damage and developed maladaptive patterns of relating as a way to cope with unnatural and abusive experiences. She should be helped to see that submissiveness is a continuation and elaboration of the original abuse of power.

Transference interpretations are made within this framework and used to elaborate the dynamics of victimization. This is an significant shift in the conceptualization of transference in the therapy relationship. In a traditional paradigm, transference interpretations are in the foreground of clinical attention; this model calls attention to transference phenomena only to highlight the dynamics of abuse or to work through blocks in the treatment of the abuse.

In addition to difficulties with self-esteem, victims of sexual violence are inhibited in their self-development (Brown and Fromm 1986). As a result of the loss of meaning and loss of belief in the future that trauma victims experience, they appear to have difficulty investing ego resources in occupational choices. Consequently, they tend to be undereducated and underemployed. Furthermore, because of emotional lability, authority problems, substance abuse, or reenactment behaviors, their employment patterns are often characterized by lack of direction and frequent job changes. Those who are able to make career commitments disproportionately tend to choose helping professions. As the negative introjects and self-representations are resolved, these women often reevaluate their life direction. The therapist should actively encourage them to reexamine long-held underestimations of their capabilities. Often, this is the first time these women have been encouraged to see themselves as competent and capable of managing responsibility. At this time, many women are often able to make new investments in themselves and will return to school or seek additional training.

Group Psychotherapy

Specialized groups are generally seen as a treatment of choice for victims of trauma (Herman and Schatzow 1984). A time-limited sexual abuse focus group, used in conjunction with individual psychotherapy and a twelve-step program, can be quite effective. The addition of group therapy toward the latter part of the integration phase allows the patient to address issues of identity and self-esteem with other group members. The group is a powerful intervention for addressing negative introjects as the patient is confronted with the distorted self-devaluations of her peers. Correcting these distortions challenges her experience of herself as defective.

The group, which meets on a weekly basis for approximately fifteen weeks, is based on the model described by Herman and Schatlow (1984). It is a problem-solving group focused on cognitive restructuring of the sexual violence from a feminist perspective and exploration of psychodynamic issues secondary to the abuse. It is intended to demystify the isolation, shame, and powerlessness experienced by abused women.

Women referred to the group meet individually with the therapist for screening and preparation for the group experience. Patients who are acting out, actively suicidal, or currently self-destructive are screened out of the group because of the impact of these behaviors on other group members. These women can benefit from group therapy in an inpatient setting, where they can be protected from self-destructive urges precipitated by the painful clinical material (Bollerud 1990). On an outpatient basis, the group experience appears to be most beneficial during the latter phase of memory and affect integration, after stabilization has been completed. Women who do not have specific memories can benefit from group therapy, as it may provoke enhanced recall. Membership can include recovering chemically dependent women, as well as women who are not substance abusing; however, members are not admitted until sobriety is firmly established. Frequently, groups will include women recovering from chemical dependency, eating disorders, and post-traumatic symptoms. All members are asked to attend every meeting and to commit themselves to the entire fifteen-week course.

There are no prohibitions about intermember contact; in fact, members are encouraged to provide support to each other. Perhaps as a part of identification with the aggressor, female victims of abuse tend to devalue themselves and other women. They are often alienated or estranged from same-sex peers. Paradoxically, they view men as sources of security and nurturance and see women as judgmental and untrustworthy. This misogyny is explored directly within the group. The women are encouraged to discuss explicitly their role as potential allies and resources for each other. Exposing and exploring this fear of other women has a powerful impact on abuse survivors. For many women, it is the first time that they have been encouraged to celebrate their feminine identity. Fostering a community of supportive women empowers them to detach from patterns of dependence on men (Bollerud 1990).

Herman and Schatzow (1984) suggest a few sessions for introduction and goal setting, followed by a number of weeks in which each group member tells her story. Setting aside one session for each member appears to provide adequate attention to each story, as well as time to process each member's reactions. As in twelve-step groups, members are encouraged to identify with each other's story rather than to criticize or give advice.

Two modifications to this model have been quite productive. The first technique was originally suggested to this author by S. Stanley (pers. com. 1987); each group member is encouraged to use photographs in the process of telling her story. She is asked to include pictures taken before, during, and after her abuse. These graphic representations often show the dramatic negative effects of abuse through changes in affective expression or body image. The patient is able to "see" her pre-abused self; this visual image is often in direct contrast to negative self-representations that have been used to justify the abuse. The patient is asked to keep a pre-abuse photograph prominently displayed at home throughout the duration of the group.

After each group member has told her story, several weeks are devoted to prominent themes that group members have in common, such as anger, sexuality, or relationship with the offender. Participants are usually asked to do homework associated with the theme; the attention during the intervening week tends to enhance the quality of the material brought to sessions.

As Bollerud (1990) noted, victimization generates profound existential doubts that leave the survivor questioning, "Why me?" Invariably, she identifies shameful aspects of herself that she believes contributed to her selection as a victim. These negative self-representations are used to rationalize the abuse. The chemically dependent woman is particularly vulnerable to this self-doubt because of ego-dystonic sexual or aggressive behaviors engaged in while intoxicated. Through group disclosure, the patient can confront and shed these feelings of alienation and humiliation. Sharing traumatic experiences fosters a reevaluation of her perception of herself as deserving abuse. In addition, the group therapist intersperses didactic explanations of the behavioral syndromes associated with sexual violence (Eth and Pynoos 1985; Walker 1984) as these topics arise.

In the final session, an expressive technique is used to help the women rid themselves of the debilitating shame that haunts so many survivors. Each participant is asked to bring in something that represents her shame and to share it with the group. These symbols can then be destroyed in a group ritual of purification. Group members have brought in body tracings, drawings, old suicide letters, and photographs. The destructions of these symbols is followed by a group celebration in which a collage of the members' pre-abuse pictures is distributed; this collection of photos is a powerful challenge to remnants of self-blame. This process appears to solidify the learnings of the group.

Summary

Many chemically dependent women present with symptoms of unresolved trauma from sexual violence. Frequently, they are locked in cycles of victimization and intoxication. Because of the similar defenses used to cope with addiction and abuse, they may be unable to break this pattern without education and treatment for both problems. A multimodal treatment strategy, utilizing twelve-step programs, individual psychotherapy, and special focus groups, may be necessary.

In approaching this treatment, a phase model of intervention is useful. In particular, when the patient is being treated on an outpatient basis, sobriety should be attained prior to efforts to elicit traumatic material. Furthermore, uncovering the trauma does not complete the working-through process. Rather, once the abuse is recalled and processed, distortions in the patient's sense of self-need to be explored and redressed. Special focus groups can be helpful at this stage of treatment.

References

American Psychiatric Association (1987). *Diagnostic and Statistical Manual of Mental Disorders* (3rd Ed., Rev.). Washington, D.C.: American Psychiatric Association.

Bollerud, K. (1990). A model for the treatment of trauma-related syndromes among chemically dependent inpatient women. *Journal of Substance Abuse Treatment* 7:83–87.

Braun, B. G. (1990). Dissociative disorders as a sequalae to incest. In R. P. Kluft (Ed.), *Incest Related Syndromes of Adult Psychopathology.* Washington, D.C.: American Psychiatric Press, pp. 227–246.

Brown, D. P., and Fromm, E. (1986). *Hypnotherapy and Hypnoanalysis.* Hillsdale, NJ: Lawrence Erlbaum.

Coleman, E. (1987). Child physical and sexual abuse among chemically dependent individuals. *Journal of Chemical Dependency Treatment* 1(1):27–39.

Courtois, C. (1988). *Healing the Incest Wound.* New York: Norton.

Eth, S., and Pynoos, R. S. (Eds.) (1985). *Post-Traumatic Stress Disorders in Children.* Washington, D.C.: American Psychiatric Press.

Evans, S., & Schaefer, S. (1987). Incest and chemically dependent women: Treatment implications. *Journal of Chemical Dependency Treatment* 1(1):141–173.

Gelinas, D. (1989, May). *Treating Survivors of Sexual Abuse.* Presentation at Cheshire Medical Center, Keene, NH.

Herman, J. (1981). *Father-Daughter Incest.* Cambridge, MA: Harvard University Press.

Herman, J., and Schatzow, E. (1984). Time-limited group therapy for women with a history of incest. *International Journal of Group Psychotherapy.* 144:908–913.

James, J. & Meyerding, J. (1977). Early sexual experiences as a factor in prostitution. *Archives of Sexual Behavior* 7:31–42.

Kovach, J. (1986). Incest as a treatment issue for alcoholic women. *Alcoholism Treatment Quarterly* 3:1–15.

Mayer, A. (1983). *Incest: A Treatment Manual for Therapy with Victims, Spouses and Offenders.* Holmes Beach, FL.: Learning Publications.

O'Neill, E. (1956). *Long Day's Journey Into Night.* New Haven, CT: Yale University Press.

Reiker, C. E. (1986). The victim-to-patient process: The disconfirmation and transformation of abuse. *American Journal of Orthopsychiatry* 56:360–370.

Ross, C. A., Norton, G. R., & Anderson, G. (1988). The dissociative experiences scale: a replication study. *Dissociation* 1:21–22.

Russell, D. (1986). *The Secret Trauma.* New York: Basic Books.

Schaefer, S., and Evans, S. (1987). Women, sexuality and the process of recovery. *Journal of Chemical Dependency Treatment* 1(1):91–120.

Terr, L. (1990). *Too Scared to Cry.* New York: Harper and Row.

van der Kolk, B. A. (1989). The compulsion to repeat the trauma: Reenactment, revictimization and masochism. *Psychiatric Clinics of North America* 12(2):389–411.

van der Kolk, B. A., and Herman, J. (1987). Traumatic antecedents of borderline personality. In B. A. van der Kolk (Ed.), *Psychological Trauma* Washington, D.C.: American Psychiatric Press, pp. 111–126.

Walker, L. E. (1984). *The Battered Women Syndrome.* New York: Springer.

Watkins, J. G. (1971). The affect bridge: a hypnoanalytic technique. *International Journal of Clinical and Experimental Hypnosis* 19:21–27.

Yandow, V. (1989). Alcoholism in women. *Psychiatric Annals* 19:243–247.

8

Inpatient Psychiatric Care for Victims of Sexual Abuse

George M. Dominiak

Included in our apothecary of clinical approaches to the treatment
of sexually traumatized individuals, alongside various alterations
in group therapy structure, hypnotic technique, couples work,
and individual psychotherapy, is the use of hospital-level psychiatric
care. Inpatient psychiatric treatment is a powerful tool that has the
potential to alter the direction of a person's outpatient treatment,
living situation, medication regimen, diagnosis, and relationships
with health care providers and insurers. Within its capacity for introducing enormous change in patients' lives lies hope for clinical
growth among the severely disturbed—and, conversely, many of its
dangers. In the case of treating trauma survivors, the dangers must
be given particular consideration. This is true because patients with
a history of sexual abuse are exquisitely sensitive to the dynamics of
power and control. Also, for them, the transfer of trust onto new or
multiple caretakers (as is usually required during hospitalization) is
a complicated process.

The modes of treatment employed in inpatient services include
creating new caring or "holding" relationships that must be shared
with other patients; intensive and potentially intrusive explorations
by many team members for the sake of assessment; limiting, containing, and shaping maladaptive behaviors; and public discussion in
group meetings. It is not surprising that misdiagnosis, insensitive application of control and force, regression, and actual or symbolic retraumatization are constant risks of hospital treatment.

For the patient, hospitalization can be experienced as an opportunity for safe respite or, conversely, as a situation in which she or
he will be controlled and manipulated arbitrarily by strangers (Kluft
1991). There are a number of necessary realities that may impinge
on the patient's sense of security as admission proceeds. An unspec-

161

ified amount of personal information that previously was private between patient and therapist will become known to a group of individuals; that is, it will become "public." The patient is also aware that details of her or his history and communications will be discussed frequently in staff meetings. Demands will be made, expectations implied, rules upon rules put forth, consequences to responding inappropriately will be administered, and all this in addition to coping with whatever crisis situation precipitated admission. The patient has very little autonomy and even less control over these new circumstances unless she or he complies.

In this context, the responsibility of the hospital staff to create a safe therapeutic environment and to foster the rapid development of some amount of trust pose a formidable clinical challenge. Given the enormity of the demands of inpatient work, it is remarkable that so little exists in the literature to help us understand better how to use the strengths of the inpatient experience to benefit abuse survivors. Sakheim, Hess and Chivas 1988, Kluft 1991, and this chapter are early attempts at sharing clinical experiences and suggestions from the perspectives of both outpatient therapists and inpatient clinicians. Sakheim, Hess, and Chivas and Kluft write specifically about the needs of individuals with multiple personality disorder. This chapter will address the larger group of sexually traumatized persons who require hospital psychiatric care. The principles described are hoped to be equally applicable to private hospital settings and general and community hospital services. For practical reasons the focus will be on brief (that is, days to weeks) rather than extensive hospital stays; most individuals in today's economy do not have the option for longer-term inpatient treatment, even if it is clinically indicated. There will also be a brief discussion of the indications, advantages, and risks of referring a patient to specialized inpatient services for treatment of various forms of traumatic stress reactions.

Use of the Hospital as a Treatment Modality: When to Admit

Outpatient clinicians vary widely in their perspectives on utilizing inpatient treatment. For some, hospitalization is used for restabilization of patients not far from baseline. The patient is seen as being in need of an opportunity to give over external controls temporarily and to gain a reprieve from the constant bombardment of traumatic memories, vacillating affect, and disruptive impulses. Other clinicians rarely hospitalize, seeing inpatient care solely as a last resort for extreme crises. Generally speaking, the threshold for seeking admission is personally determined. How it affects treatment expectations and if it relates consistently with other practices regarding professional boundaries, therapist availability, use of other community resources, and the influence of managed care reviewers obviously is clinically important.

Patients who have lived in environments where safety and trust are unpredictably and at times brutally violated often develop a keen sensitivity to the control dynamics and behavioral expectations of their caretakers. They can sense disappointment, distancing, or rejuvenated hope. How the therapist genuinely feels about her or his patient being hospitalized, whether it is relief, outrage, or some other sentiment, is almost always significant to the therapeutic relationship. Consistency and reasonableness are recommended as guiding principles. Above all, hospitalization should make sense to both patient and therapist.

From the perspective of inpatient clinicians, the indications for hospitalization of sexual abuse survivors are not significantly different from those for other patients. Escalating suicidal ideation, non-lethal self mutilation of increasing frequency (or other behavioral dyscontrol unresponsive to outpatient intervention), brief psychotic reactions, exacerbation of mood disorder, incapacitating anxiety, diagnostic evaluation and consultation, medication trials, and/or implementation of hypnotic or amytal interviews with high-risk patients are the most common nonspecific reasons for admission.

There are, in addition, indications that are particular to trauma pathology and the working through of traumatic experiences. These would include the need for abreaction, affective cognitive and behavioral dyscontrol resulting from remembering previously repressed abuse events, disorganization from dissociative mechanisms, the many vicissitudes of multiple personality disorder, reevaluation of complicated medication regimens, treatment of exacerbated multi-syndrome clinical states such as major depression and panic with intensification of dissociative defenses, and the de-escalation of transference-countertransference binds. In summary, given the limits of a patient's social supports, if she or he becomes unsafe and there is potential or actual dangerous loss of control, hospitalization is generally seen as warranted.

There also exists a small group of patients who require multiple brief hospitalizations at crucial periods in their treatment. In the past, these individuals would have been referred to long term or specialized inpatient care but do not have access to such services in current times because of finances or lack of availability. I have known patients who have spent the equivalent of six or seven months in a hospital over a twelve-month period via multiple stays of one to five weeks each in length. These individuals typically are highly unstable, quick to threaten self-injury, or in the midst of surfacing new memories of horrific abuse experiences and in need of a safe environment for abreaction and restabilization of adaptive defenses. More often than not, they are also particularly interesting or likable patients. Disruption of outpatient clinical teams or entrusted social supports are common precipitants for admission.

For this group of patients, hospitalization is seen not only as quieting crisis situations but additionally as facilitating critical nodal points in a long-term outpatient treatment plan. Though it might appear that the purpose of each hospitalization is for mitigating acute exacerbations of symptoms, the goals of the overall treatment are longitudinal and rehabilitative in focus, essentially as though the patient were in long-term inpatient care. Often, inpatient services will develop close working relationships with outpatient treaters to maintain continuity in caretakers, psychopharmacology, and philosophy of approach. The patients would otherwise circulate from one hospital to another, disrupting the potential for developing cohesive treatment planning and intervention.

On the other hand, gaining hospital admission is not always a simple matter. Trauma survivors are not openly welcomed under all circumstances. Inpatient services might refuse admission of an abuse survivor, even when hospitalization is indicated, if their current patient population is taxing the staff significantly, if they have had particularly unsuccessful or ungratifying experiences with that patient in the past, or if there are one or more abuse perpetrators on the ward and the staff has not had adequate experience managing such a patient mix.

For the therapist, the administrative task of arranging for hospitalization can be particularly frustrating and ungratifying, not to mention costly time-wise. Since patients in general are reluctant to be hospitalized, therapists often expend considerable effort preparing them for admission. Hearing about a rejection for admission or even the cumbersome process of waiting for hours for insurance clearance or approval by managed care reviewers may reinforce the patient's ambivalence about hospitalization, potentially compounding hopelessness about being able to get help. This may further complicate the clinical work. Out of frustration, the therapist might finally refer the patient to a local hospital emergency service and hope for the best. In this case, both the therapist and the patient hand over personal control to others.

Getting the Most Out of Hospitalization: "Preparing" the Inpatient Treatment

We know from experience that severely abused individuals in psychotherapy of any type often require special attention and consideration. The most disturbed of trauma survivors are predictably inconsistent in their manner of presentation. Herman, Perry, and van der Kolk (1989), Goodwin, Cheeves, and Connell (1990) and Perry et al. (1990) document well the varied clinical manifestations of these patients, the misguided diagnoses applied, and the sometimes convoluted clinical interventions imposed in the guise of treatment. Consistency in approaching the management and understanding of a patient who may show different aspects of her or his personality, mood, anxieties, and needs while overall showing the potential for self-injury or destruction is an obvious recommendation. Regardless of its conceptual simplicity, coordination of inpatient and outpatient treatments somehow remains enormously difficult to execute.

Like any other professionals, we as mental health clinicians are a capable, educated, and opinionated lot. We trust our observations and generally have considerable experience making clinical decisions in relative isolation. To some extent, this leads us to learn to overvalue our knowledge and judgments, in particular as they relate to our long-term patients. Often this side effect to individual practice is, for certain patients, directly proportional to how responsible we feel for managing their safety and stability.

Inpatient treatment teams, under pressure to create and manage a safe clinical environment, commonly struggle against the tendency to make clinical decisions on the basis of a given staff member's singular opinions or observations. Because of the ability of abused patients to present equally intense and therefore believable aspects of themselves to different staff, everyone, including the most experienced hospital clinician, is vulnerable to overvaluation of her or his personal "therapeutic" beliefs.

Perhaps the most important task facing an inpatient treatment system is the development of consistency in clinical management.

Most commonly, this is accomplished by the treatment teams working together to develop a sense of solidarity in clinical beliefs about the needs of particular patients or diagnostic subgroups of patients. Inpatient units thrive on generating and propagating an air of consensus. Though it would be easy to criticize such a homogenizing process, it is important to understand that it is essential to maintaining organization and competence in the inpatient team as a working group. To the outsider, interacting with such a group can leave one feeling that the team is inflexible or limited in their scope. In fact, some treatment services are quite rigid in their beliefs and treatment approach; however, this does not preclude their potential usefulness for certain patients.

If the organizational dynamics and needs of inpatient psychiatric treatment services can be appreciated as such and respected by outpatient therapists, the awareness can be utilized to facilitate collaboration of clinical efforts. Unfortunately, it appears that the burden of responsibility in coordinating inpatient and outpatient treatments lies initially with the outpatient clinician. Ideally, she or he would undergo some preparatory negotiation and clarification with the inpatient team representative regarding the treatment as soon in the admission process as is possible.

The nature of the extent of activity necessary in preparing the inpatient treatment team is determined by how well the service knows the patient and how much experience they have had in working with the therapist. If the patient is well-known and the therapist familiar, then only a minor realignment may be necessary, such as updates on recent events, changes in the patient's clinical status, and reaffirmations about the parameters of the therapist's involvement with the patient and team during hospitalization. There are, however, a few suggestions to be made.

The first, mentioned above, is that the therapist should try to engage representatives of the inpatient service as colleagues in the clinical work. Secondly, clinical history must be shared, including information about previous experiences the patient may have had in hospital settings (that is, what the team may expect from the patient regarding self-control, compliance, and trustworthiness regarding safety). Thirdly, there should be as clear a communication as possible regarding the purpose for hospitalization and anticipated diagnostic and/or treatment goals. Fourth, the treatment team will benefit from clarification regarding the needs of the therapist. This would include the extent of the therapist's involvement in treatment planning, how often and under what circumstances she or he wishes to be called, clarification of who the team contact person(s) will be, and the nature and frequency of visits or phone interactions with the hospitalized patient.

Preparing the Patient for Hospitalization

Trauma survivors should be given some general information regarding the therapist's activities in the admission process. Additionally, they should be given clarification regarding the extent of the therapist's involvement in treatment during the hospital stay. It can be quite reassuring for the patient to hear that the trusted outpatient therapist will be active in inpatient treatment planning. Also, clarity regarding the availability of the outpatient therapist and the limitations regarding contact while in the hospital is typically helpful. In any case, consideration should be given to the patient's potential reactions regarding hospitalization. Some examples would include fears of being abandoned by the therapist, growing hopelessness about ever getting better, being forced to face memories and feelings that will be overwhelming, expectations of retraumatization, and thoughts of being seen by the therapist as having failed (which seem validated by the need for hospitalization). Though the patient's beliefs about themselves and the "true" motives of the therapist and hospital staff cannot be changed, explaining that such reactions might be expected and welcoming exploration about them can be calming.

Unfortunately, many abuse victims are in crisis at the time of admission, unable to hear or share. Obviously, if the patient is absolutely overwhelmed with affect, impulses, or fragmentation of consciousness or thought process, the therapist's task changes. Understanding and verbal communication is superseded temporarily by the need to keep the patient safe and to place her or him in an environment that could modulate external or internal overstimulation and foster the return of self-control. In crisis situations, it is important to respect the patient's physical and interpersonal boundaries and to maintain personal integrity. Even if physical restraint cannot be avoided, this intervention should be treated as a clinical intervention in a manner that does not add to the humiliation, degradation, and hostility inherent in the act.

In the heat of the clinical crisis, steady, calming, orienting communication by a familiar or soft voice is most helpful. Only after the patient is in a safe setting and under better control can discussion about the experience become fruitful. It is surprising how much detail is remembered by many of our most out-of-control or actively dissociating patients when allowed to reflect back to their treatment in crisis situations. This is surprising because, at the time, they seemed psychologically unreachable. It appears that during crises, when the patient cannot self-regulate behavior, thought, or affect and cannot communicate to verify or describe their experience, the capacity to perceive, feel, and hear our activity is often preserved.

The Psychiatric Inpatient Setting

Inpatient treatment services that may be similar in structure, organization, and purpose to many other inpatient services may differ widely in the nature of the professional and social milieu they provide. In part, this may account for some of the difficulty in making research comparisons between treatment settings. The personal characteristics of staff members, clinical traditions of the institution in which the unit is found, and the social environment created by the patient group at any given point in time determine the nature of the clinical milieu. These variables also account for changes in how the service might be experienced by observers or patients returning to the setting at different times.

The potential benefits and hazards of hospital treatment are many. Which gain prominence during hospitalization is determined by the "fit" of patient needs and the staff's capabilities during the treatment. It is well-known that the inpatient environment and the work of the hospital treatment team have a clear and powerful influence. We have all seen how some patients show dramatic remission of symptoms within days of entering the hospital. They appear to respond to the "holding" experience of the inpatient milieu with diminution in impulsivity and anxiety, an improvement in self-care functions such as eating and grooming, or increased tolerance of social contact. This occurs most commonly when the patient has developed a relationship with the staff from previous admissions. A possible danger in the treatment of familiar patients on short-term inpatient services is the development of a passive clinical attitude that may result in a stagnation in creative treatment planning. This impedes the process of growth and change while appearing to be consistent and supportive.

For other patients, hospitalization initially threatens rather than soothes. Such individuals may quickly regress into struggles with staff focused on privacy, self-destructive behavior, staff insensitivities, unit regulations, attendance at meetings, and medication compliance, among other issues, as will be discussed below. The outcome in cases such as these often includes an unfortunate polarization among staff, a growing intolerance of the patient and rigidification of expectations. In essence, psychological battle lines are drawn, fueled by hostility and control dynamics. Such situations require an immediate case review involving all team members as well as including input from the patient.

Complicating the process of engaging the patient in the hospital is the fact that many severely disturbed abuse victims are extremely sensitive to external controls. As Kluft (1991) writes, "Most MPD (multiple personality disorder) patients will initially perceive even the most gentle constraints and limit settings as punitive and the most minimal redirections as critical" (p. 711). Even in cases when such reactions consist of demands and accusations that are clearly transference reactions or minimally based in reality, it is exceedingly difficult to manage the situation in a manner that sensitively modulates the patient's responses while maintaining a sense of integrity among the inpatient staff. Psychodynamic understanding from whatever school of thought you choose is only rarely useful in such circumstances when the "clinical moment" is filled with immediate interpersonal tension and conflict and occurs on the ward with unfamiliar staff, outside the safeguarding structure of a therapy session.

The task for the staff in such situations is to regroup and attempt to be consistent in the expectations and regulations imposed on the patient, including the patient as much as possible in the treatment planning. This lessens the chance that the patient will be surprised time and again by new external constraints that seem arbitrarily determined. Outpatient therapists should expect to hear strong reports of terrible experiences from their patients, and families should be forewarned of the possibility. Often, experienced staffs will alert the therapist or significant others to anticipate calls of complaint and suggest that they reserve judgment when the calls come, maintaining a supportive, caring perspective with the patient but contacting the staff as soon as possible to help integrate the realities of the situation with potential distortions. Inadequate communication with the inpatient team paves the way to unnecessary animosity ("splitting") that may further lead to disruptions in the progress of the treatment.

For the most part, a psychiatric inpatient service offers safety, structure, personal attention, provision of basic needs (food, recreation, sometimes clothing), and the opportunity for renewing or developing supportive social contact. Additionally, it provides the expected diagnostic and therapeutic treatment interventions. For patients recovering from sexual traumatization, however, those components of inpatient treatment that generally facilitate healing can be felt to be harmful. For example, the pressure to share difficulties publicly in treatment groups to gain support can readily induce shame. The tendency of inpatient treatment to validate the presence of severe pathology and limitations in functioning can devastate self-esteem. The requirement to subject oneself cooperatively to the expectations of others (including staff) can regenerate a sense of powerlessness or revictimization. Also, being sequestered in a hospital away from stressful circumstances or abusive partners can paradoxically stimulate the experience of abandonment and extreme isolation or, in some cases, even a depersonalization or dissociative reaction in response to the unfamiliarity of the inpatient setting.

Hospital services experienced in managing the sensitivities of abused individuals can usually successfully compensate for the potential dangers. Caring, unintrusive attempts at contact, allowances for self-regulating safety behaviors such as time alone or contact with outside supports, appropriately sharing responsibility in decision making, and involving the patient in treatment planning appear to be helpful.

Because most patients enter the hospital during a crisis or in a condition of compromised self-control, initial clinical interventions focus on supporting adaptive defenses, self-soothing, and regaining the ability to tolerate and self-regulate anxiety, affect, and cognitive process. Periods of abreaction, sometimes quite demonstrative, may be necessary before controls are recovered. Gentle, clear, and understanding (but at times directive) personal contact is essential. Often, it is helpful to separate out administrative decision making in a clinician's role from her or his assessment and therapeutic functions, that is, to create a therapist/administrator or so-called T/A split. In this case, the "therapist" would not hold the role of decision maker regarding privileges. The dynamic of control is removed from that relationship, and the patient may then feel the therapy meetings are a safer place for sharing difficult material. The tendency to react to any controls as punishment is thus circumvented rather than confronted.

An unfortunate characteristic of unlocked or "open" inpatient services is that overt emotional reactions are generally not well tolerated. As patients abreact, they are often quickly labeled as unmanageable and transferred to a more secure setting, thus disrupting the developing patient-staff relationship. Many times, if patients can be safely held for twenty-four or forty-eight hours while abreacting or in a temporary state of dyscontrol, they calm down and the work can proceed with a reinforcement of the treatment relationship resulting from having shared the crisis.

On more secure or locked units, the tolerance for emotional reactions is generally higher; however, the environments on such services are typically disruptive and threatening because of the severity of pathology in other patients. Services specializing in treating abuse victims have an advantage in this regard.

Inpatient management of traumatized individuals requires that frequent and often rapid clinical judgments be made. Staff discussion about treatment decisions and careful supervision by experienced clinicians are essential elements of good care. We know that the immediate needs of trauma victims can shift fairly dramatically. The need of the inpatient staff to have sensible consistency in approach can clash directly with this. As an example, for some patients, emotional outbursts are gratuitous and regressive, whereas for others they are elements of the necessary working through of newly recollected traumatic memories. Distinguishing between the two requires considerable sophistication. Deciding that no outbursts are acceptable is a common treatment approach that equalizes clinical intervention but negates individual differences. Not all inpatient services can manage significant variability in treatment planning for their patients, and this limitation should be appreciated and respected. Attempts at overextending the capabilities of an inpatient service rarely lead to fruitful outcomes without extensive planning.

Other difficult decisions facing inpatient treaters may cross the boundary between clinical empathy and ethical issues. For example, there are patients who may ask for physical restraint even when not in apparent dyscontrol because of the soothing experience they describe gaining from it. Such a request typically comes at night when the therapist is unavailable to the patient or staff for consultation. Should the staff comply? This is another instance where clinical theory is not particularly helpful in practical decision making. For example, we know from the work of van der Kolk (1989) of the compulsion of traumatized persons to recreate elements of their trauma in their immediate environments: "Many traumatized people expose themselves, seemingly compulsively, to situations reminiscent of the original trauma. These behavioral reenactments are rarely consciously understood to be related to earlier life experiences" (pp. 389–90).

Is allowing the restraint actually allowing an attempt at self-soothing? Should the request be respected as an example of the patient taking more adaptive control of destructive impulses, or would permission to use restraint upon request inadvertently recreate elements of abuse experiences? How would the patient understand the decision at a later time? Would it be best to have a general policy that says no to such a request under any circumstances? What are the risks of enforcing this kind of policy blindly?

There are no easy answers to these questions (and others like them) regarding clinical decisions about patient requests or treatment interventions that face hospital clinicians on a daily basis. Generally, the more information the staff has about the individual patient's past responses to specific methods, the easier it will be for them to make difficult decisions. Also, ongoing staff education in various techniques of self-soothing, stress management, distraction, reality testing, and affect modulation will help them to provide patients with alternate means of self-regulation during difficult moments.

Among the responsibilities facing the inpatient treatment team caring for severely disturbed sexually abused patients, perhaps the most difficult include carefully maintaining awareness of personal reactions to the patients and how these reactions influence decision making. Developing a professional relationship with an abuse victim can be emotionally trying. Hearing recollections of brutal abuse is itself relatively traumatizing to clinicians (McCann and Pearlman 1990); it would be nearly impossible not to react emotionally to the patient's recollections. In addition, patients with severe disturbance challenge the clinician with life-and-death conflicts and paradoxical impulses to self-sooth via self-mutilation or self-destruction (van der Kolk 1989). Nontherapist inpatient clinicians who spend many hours with patients should not be expected to function as therapists or to react as therapists might. The fresh observations offered by frontline staff are typically unfettered by the constraints of the patient-therapist relationship and usually present a practical perspective.

Common reactions to treating abused patients include repulsion, anxiety, blaming, denial, disbelief, overprotectiveness, pity/sympathy, overreactivity to the patient's behavior, and a need to control rigidly either the patient or the patient's immediate environment. These are essentially normal reactions for an individual in a caretaking role working closely with sexually traumatized persons. Adequate supervision and educational and general collegial support are essential to maintain morale and prevent burnout. Without the opportunity to share reactions with coworkers and supervisors, these emotional responses can grow to the extent that judgment may be compromised and the process of team management is impeded.

It is strongly recommended that outpatient therapists, especially during times of disagreement, respond to the suggestions/decisions of inpatient treatment teams with compassion and understanding. No short-term inpatient psychiatric service will be able to replicate the knowledge, awareness, empathy, and support offered to the patient by her or his long-term outpatient psychotherapist. The best insurance for a good outcome to hospital treatment is beginning with realistic expectations and maintaining openness to learning from alternative perspectives and the observations of others.

Conclusion

Psychiatric hospitalization is a powerful and at times necessary intervention in the treatment of patients who have suffered sexual traumatization. For outpatient therapists, it provides their patients with opportunities for stemming the tide of self-destructive dyscontrol, careful diagnostic review, and treatment interventions in a controlled and relatively safe environment.

On the other hand, inpatient clinicians have the enormous responsibility of managing considerable legal and social power and control over the basic human rights of individuals in their care in a manner that is supportive of psychological stabilization and growth. Having such power and control cuts to the heart of the sensitivities of many sexually traumatized patients.

The challenge of exercising control and containment in a way that minimizes the experience of revictimization and that is fair to patients of many diagnoses is formidable. For this reason, some institutions have designed specialized inpatient services for the sexually abused. Various of these have been designated "women's units," "centers for abuse survivors," "dissociative disorders services," "MPD (multiple personality disorder) units," and so forth. Their advantages lie in a keen awareness of the needs of abused persons with significant psychopathology and in programming that addresses these needs specifically. The disadvantages may be that such services can overemphasize a singular clinical approach, practice diagnostic reductionism and mislabel patients, or overemphasize specific elements of psychopathology. Ideally, regardless of the site, all treatments for the sexually abused would be patient specific rather than treatment or program specific, and they would all work toward reinforcing the long-term rehabilitative goals of outpatient psychotherapy.

In summary, from the limited few topics relevant to inpatient treatment reviewed in this chapter, perhaps one should be repeated: the importance of communication and collaboration between outpatient and inpatient clinicians. Not surprisingly, it appears that developing functional and supportive professional relationships sets the path toward realistic clinical planning and effective implementation.

References

Goodwin, J. M., Cheeves, K., and Connell, V. (1990). Borderline and other severe symptoms in adult survivors of incestuous abuse. *Psychiatric Annals* 20(1):22–32.

Herman, J. L., Perry, J. C., and van der Kolk, B. A. (1989). Childhood trauma in borderline personality disorder. *American Journal of Psychiatry* 146(4):490–95.

Kluft, R. P. (1991). Hospital treatment of multiple personality disorder: An overview. *Psychiatric Clinics of North America* 14(3):695–719.

McCann, L., & Pearlman, L. A. (1990). Vicarious traumatization: A framework for understanding the psychological effects of working with victims. *Journal of Traumatic Stress* 3:131–49.

Perry, J. C., Herman, J. L., van der Kolk, B. A., Hoke, L. A. (1990). Psychotherapy and psychological trauma in borderline personality disorder. *Psychiatric Annals* 20(1):33–43.

Sakheim, D. K., Hess, E. P., & Chivas, A. (1988). General principles for short-term inpatient work with multiple personality disorder patients. *Psychotherapy* 25:117–24.

van der Kolk, B. A. (1989). The compulsion to repeat the trauma: Reenactment, revictimization, and masochism. *Psychiatric Clinics of North America* 12(2):389–411.

Acknowledgments

We all offer our gratitude to the survivors who have shared their stories with us and the readers of this book. We are especially grateful to the many professional colleagues and literary friends who have supported this publication. We wish to thank Cynthia Conrad, M.D., for sharing her expertise in the field of psychiatry and reviewing the chapter on psychopharmacology. We would like to acknowledge Stephanie Nurenberg, Ph.D., for her empathic and clinical support with the chapters on suicide and defenses. We express our appreciation to Sebern Fisher, M.A., Sylvia Rubin, M.A., Jeffery Lapid, Ph.D., and Mary Kenefick, M.S.W., for reviewing specific chapters and providing feedback. Special thanks go to Myra Gross, B.A., Margaret Nichols, Psy.D., Jack Nichols, Psy.D., Deany Andersen, Joan McGinnis, and Gail LaScola.

Index

shame due to, 3–6, 13
suicidality and, 3, 5, 6, 8,
    10, 11, 13, 14
Classical conditioning, 135,
    136–37
Clomipramine (Anafranil), 96,
    102
Clonazepam (Klonopin), 93,
    106
Clonidine, 104
Cognition
    dissociative and/or hypnotic
        states and, 64
    encapsulated, 69–70
Compulsion to repeat, 39–40
Concentration, disruption of,
    65
Conditioned stimuli (CS), 135
Conditioning
    classical, 135, 136–37
    operant, 117
Control, sensitivity to abuse of,
    18
Conversion, 40–42
Coping skills, 135–36
Cult, victimization by, 53, 59
Cultural factors in attachment
    dynamics, 26

D

Damaged-goods syndrome, 5
Daydreaming, 43
Defense mechanisms, 35–57
    acting out, 37–39
    altruism, 51–52
    against childhood
        victimization, 13, 35–
        36
    compulsion to repeat, 39–40

conversion, 40–42
denial, 22–23, 36, 42–43,
    47
disavowal, 36
dissociation. *See*
    Dissociation
humor, 52
main function of, 35
minimizing, 47–49
projection, 49, 117
regression, 36, 67–68, 124–
    25
repression, 42, 49–51,
    70
splitting, 46–47, 69
sublimation, 53
suppression, 53–54
in women, 37
Denial, 36, 42–43, 47
    style of attachment dynamics
        and, 22–23
Depersonalization, 45–46, 67,
    146
Depression(s)
    with agitation, 95–96
    defined, 94
    despair episodes, 97
    melancholic, 95
    neurovegetative, 95
    psychopharmacology of, 94–
        98
Depressive symptoms, 90
Derealization, 46, 146
Derepression, 51
Desipramine (Norpramin),
    92
Despair, 97
Devaluation, sexual, 154
Developmental tasks, sexual
    trauma and, 124

About the Authors

Shanti Shapiro, M.S.W., is a psychiatric social worker in private practice in Springfield, Massachusetts. She has worked at the Institute of Living, Four Winds Hospital, and several outpatient settings. Ms. Shapiro provides consultation and training and presents at national conferences. She has specialized in the field of sexual abuse for over twelve years. Ms. Shapiro completed her B.A. at the University of Massachusetts and continued her education at the Smith College School for Social Work. She is a member of The National Association of Social Workers and the International Society for the Study of Multiple Personality and Dissociation.

George M. Dominiak, M.D., is Assistant Chairman in Psychiatry at the Mount Auburn Hospital in Cambridge, Massachusetts. He is Instructor in Psychiatry at the Harvard Medical School and is on the faculty of the Cambridge Hospital. He is also currently the book review editor of the journal *General Hospital Psychiatry*. Dr. Dominiak is a graduate of Haverford College and Harvard Medical School. He completed his psychiatric training at the Yale Residency in Psychiatry; afterward, he served as assistant unit director of the Inpatient Service for the Treatment of Borderline and Other Severe Personality Disorders in the Long-Term Division of New York Hospital, Westchester Division. He has also been program director of Young Adult and Eating-Disorder Services at Four Winds Hospital in Katonah, New York.

About the Contributors

Kathleen Bollerud, Ed.D., is certified as a psychologist and addictions specialist. She received her doctorate from Harvard University in Cambridge, Massachusetts. Dr. Bollerud was the director of psychology at Beech Hill Hospital in Dublin, New Hampshire, where she developed a model for the treatment of trauma-related syndromes among chemically dependent women. She currently maintains a private practice in Keene, New Hampshire, specializing in the treatment of victims of sexual violence. Dr. Bollerud provides clinical consultation and training to agencies and practitioners on issues related to substance abuse and trauma. She is a member of the American Professional Society on the Abuse of Children, the Society for Traumatic Stress Studies, and the International Society for the Study of Multiple Personality and Dissociation.

Barbara G. Orrok, M.D., graduated from the University of California School of Medicine in San Francisco and completed psychiatric residency at Yale University. She received training in substance abuse research and treatment at the University of Connecticut and the Institute of Living and is currently on the faculty at Yale, where she is medical director of an inpatient detoxification service and an outpatient alcoholism treatment clinic. Dr. Orrok is interested in women's issues in psychiatry and is studying the impact of pregnancy on psychotherapy.

Elizabeth P. Hess, Ph.D., is a clinical psychologist with more than ten years of experience in evaluating and treating persons suffering from dissociative disorders and post-traumatic stress disorders. She obtained her training at Stanford, the University of California at

Berkeley, and the University of Montana, where she studied clinical hypnosis with John G. Watkins and Helen Watkins. She has published and led workshops and provides presentations for the New England chapter of the International Society for the Study of Multiple Personality and Dissociation, Seminars for Professional Advancement, Tufts University Medical School, and other groups. She specializes in the use of hypnosis and the diagnosis and treatment of dissociative disorders.